LEADERSHIP:

The ASTD Trainer's Sourcebook

Elaine Biech
CREATIVITY: THE ASTD TRAINER'S SOURCEBOOK

Anne F. Coyle
LEADERSHIP: THE ASTD TRAINER'S SOURCEBOOK

Dennis C. Kinlaw
COACHING: THE ASTD TRAINER'S SOURCEBOOK

Dennis C. Kinlaw
FACILITATION SKILLS: THE ASTD TRAINER'S SOURCEBOOK

Herbert R. Miller
SALES: THE ASTD TRAINER'S SOURCEBOOK

Tina Rasmussen
DIVERSITY: THE ASTD TRAINER'S SOURCEBOOK

Judson Smith
QUALITY: THE ASTD TRAINER'S SOURCEBOOK

Cresencio Torres & Deborah M. Fairbanks
TEAMBUILDING: THE ASTD TRAINER'S SOURCEBOOK

Bobette Hayes Williamson
SUPERVISION: THE ASTD TRAINER'S SOURCEBOOK

John C. Wills
STRATEGIC PLANNING: THE ASTD TRAINER'S SOURCEBOOK

LEADERSHIP:

The ASTD Trainer's Sourcebook

Anne F. Coyle, Ph.D.

McGraw-Hill

New York   San Francisco   Washington D.C.   Auckland   Bogotá
Caracas   Lisbon   London   Madrid   Mexico City   Milan
Montreal   New Delhi   San Juan   Singapore
Sydney   Tokyo   Toronto

Library of Congress Catalog Card Number: 96-78874

McGraw-Hill

A Division of The McGraw·Hill Companies

4 5 6 7 8 9   MAL/MAL   0 1

ISBN 0-07-053439-X

Sourcebook Team:

Co-Publishers:	Philip Ruppel, Training McGraw-Hill
	Nancy Olson, American Society for Training and Development
Acquisitions Editor:	Richard Narramore, Training McGraw-Hill
Editing Supervisor:	Paul R. Sobel, McGraw-Hill Professional Book Group
Production Supervisor:	Donald F. Schmidt, McGraw-Hill Professional Book Group
Series Advisor:	Richard L. Roe
Series Managing Editor:	Anne F. Coyle, Ph.D.
Editing/Production:	Deborah Stockton, DOS Enterprises; Bill McLaughlin, Advanced Communications; Kalista Johnston-Nash

Contents

Preface . . . . *xi*

1. Introduction **1**

   Sourcebook Organization 2

      Workshop Building Blocks 4

      Subject/Reference Matrix 5

      Time Block/Methods Matrix 7

      Navigating the Training Plans 8

      Understanding the Icons 9

      Sample Page 10

2. Background **11**

   Why Leadership? 12

   What Is Leadership? 12

   Leadership Characteristics Chart 13

   Leadership Characteristics 14

   Creating Followership 15

   Leader's Source of Power 16

   Leadership Differences 16

   Leaders Are Good Communicators 18

   Characteristic #1: Question Groupthink 19

   Characteristic #2: Reset Direction 21

   Characteristic #3: Guide Cooperative Actions 25

   Characteristic #4: Walk the Talk 28

   Characteristic #5: Motivate Others—
        Extrinsic Vs. Intrinsic Motivation 29

   Encouraging the Individual Team Member 29

   Credit Effort and Risk Taking 31

   Create Team Environment 31

3. Workshop Preparation **35**

   Designing Your Own Training Program 36

      Defining Client Needs 36

      Determining Program Content 36

   Selecting Training Methods and Media 38

      Training Methods 38

      Keep Spotlight Moving 40

      Getting Ready 41

      Announce the Session 41

Certificate of Completion 43
Prepare for the Session 43
Participant Roster 43
Preparation Checklist 45
Equipment 46
Workshop Agenda Template 47
Participant Roster Worksheet 48
Room Setup 49

Facilitator Preparation 51
On Day of the Workshop 51
Conducting the Workshop 51
Workshop Follow-Up 55
Certificate of Achievement 56
Leadership Workshop Tent Card 57

4.   One-Day Leadership Workshop **59**

Purpose and Objectives 59

Workshop Agendas 60

Materials Needed 62

Suggested Flipcharts 63
Building the Vision 63
Preferred Emphasis 63
Slogans 64
Behaviors 64
Milestones 64
Celebration Ideas 64

Training Plan 65
1   Introduction to the Workshop (8:00 to 9:00) 65
2   What Is Leadership? (9:00 to 10:10) 68
3   It Starts with a Vision (10:10 to 11:15) 71
4   People Make It Happen (11:15 to 1:45) 75
5   Demonstrating Commitment (1:45 to 2:45) 79
6   Motivating the Team (2:45 to 4:15) 82
7   Personal Commitment (4:15 to 4:45) 86

5.   Half-Day Leadership Workshop **87**

Purpose and Objectives 87

Workshop Agenda 88

Materials Needed 89

Suggested Flipcharts 90
Building the Vision 90
Preferred Emphasis 90
It's Up to You 90

Keeping Vision Alive 90
Training Plan 91
   1   Introduction to the Workshop (8:00 to 9:00) 91
   2   Questioning Groupthink (9:00 to 10:15) 94
   3   Develop a Vision (10:15 to 11:55) 98

6. One-Hour Leadership Workshop **103**
  Purpose and Objectives 103
  Workshop Agenda 104
  Materials Needed 104
  Suggested Flipcharts 105
     Welcome 105
     Scope of This Session 105
  Training Plan *105*
     Giving Credit 105

7. Participant Handouts **109**
  Leadership Characteristics 110
     Leader Practices 110
  A Leader I've Known 112
  Recognizing Leadership 113
  Types of Leaders 115
     Management and Leadership 116
  Openness and Vision 117
  Leaders Learn by Listening 119
  How Vision Develops 121
  How to Communicate the Vision 123
  Roles and Responsibilities 125
  Tailor Your Coaching 126
  Training the Team 128
  Autonomy and Control 129
  Motivating the Team 130
     Intrinsic and Extrinsic Motivation 130
  Encouraging the Individual Team Member 131
  Giving Positive Feedback 132
  Giving Constructive Feedback 133
  Opportunities to Celebrate Success 134
  Commitment and Follow-Up 135

8. Learning Activities **137**
  Life Path Activity Guidelines 138
     Life Path 139

Figures of Speech Activity Guidelines 140
    Images Are Everywhere 141
Favorite Things Activity Guidelines 142
    A Few of My Favorite Things 143
Values Activity Guidelines 145
It's Up to Us to Decide 146
    My Values 148
Vision Activity Guidelines 149
Which One Is a Vision 150
Preferences Activity Guidelines 152
    Finding Out People's Preferences 153
Visualization Activity Guidelines 154
Risk Taking Activity Guidelines 156
    I Think I Can 157
Signaling Activity Guidelines 158
    You're Signaling 159
Constructive Feedback Role Play Guidelines 160
    Giving Constructive Feedback 161
Crediting Role Play Guidelines 162
    Giving Credit 163

9. Instruments and Assessments **165**
Leadership Assessment Guidelines 166
Leadership Assessment (Other) 167
Leadership Assessment (Self) 168
Paradigm Self-Assessment Guidelines 170
    Paradigm Self-Assessment 171
Listening Assessment Guidelines 172
    Listening Self-Assessment 173
    Listening Assessment (Other) 174
Coaching Assessment Guidelines 176
    Coaching Assessment Questionnaire 177
    Interview Guide 178
Goal Setting Self-Assessment Guidelines 179
    Leadership Characteristics 180
Information Gathering Mode Assessment Guidelines 182
    Information Gathering (Self) 183
Opportunities to Celebrate Assessment Guidelines 185
    Opportunities to Celebrate Successes 186

10. Overhead Transparencies **189**
    One-Day Leadership Workshop 190
    A Half-Day Leadership Workshop 191
    A One-Hour Leadership Workshop 192
    Leadership Characteristics 193
    Giving Positive Feedback 194
    Agenda and Logistics 195
    Vision Defined 196
    Communicate the Vision 197
    Build on Strengths 198
    Autonomy and Control 199
    Motivate the Team 200

Appendix **201**
    Resources for Training Professionals 201
      Books 201
      Videos 203
      Assessments 203
    Glossary 205

Index **207**

Preface

I'd like to tell you how this series came about. As a longtime editor and resource person in the training and development field, I was frequently asked by trainers, facilitators, consultants, and instructors to provide them with training designs on a variety of topics. These customers wanted one-hour, half-day, and full-day programs on such topics as team-building, coaching, diversity, supervision, and sales. Along with the training designs, they required facilitator notes, participant handouts, flipchart ideas, games, activities, structured experiences, overhead transparencies, and instruments. But, that wasn't all. They wanted to be able to reproduce, customize, and adapt these materials to their particular needs—at no cost!

Later, as an independent editor, I shared these needs with Nancy Olson, the publisher at the American Society for Training and Development. Nancy mentioned that ASTD received many similar calls from facilitators who were looking for a basic library of reproducible training materials. Many of the classic training volumes, such as Newstrom and Scannell's *Games Trainers Play* provided a variety of useful activities. However, they lacked training designs, handouts, overheads, and instruments—and, most importantly, they tended to be organized by method rather than by topic. You can guess the rest of the story: Welcome to *The ASTD Trainer's Sourcebook*.

This sourcebook is part of an open-ended series that covers the training topics most often found in many organizations. Instead of locking you into a prescribed "workbook mentality," this sourcebook will free you from having to buy more workbooks each time you present training. This volume contains everything you need—background information on the topic, facilitator notes, training designs, participant handouts, activities, instruments, flipcharts, overheads, and resources—and it's all reproducible! We welcome you to adapt it to your particular needs. Please read the copyright limitations on page iv, then photocopy…edit… add your name…add your client's name. Please don't tell us… it isn't necessary! Enjoy.

Richard L. Roe
ASTD Sourcebook Series Advisor

Chapter One:

Introduction

Welcome to *Leadership: The ASTD Trainer's Sourcebook.* We hope that you will find this a valuable tool to supplement your training in *leadership, quality, creativity, coaching, project management, time management, etc.* This complete resource package allows you to train both new and experienced leaders who work in: traditional industrial or service settings, entrepreneurial enterprises, ad hoc groups, or voluntary organizations.

This Chapter

...describes the contents and structure of the book. It will assist you in navigating through the book, selecting the building blocks needed to run one of the sessions outlined here, or creating your own training design. Major topics are:

"Sourcebook Organization " on page 2

"Workshop Building Blocks " on page 4

"Subject/Reference Matrix " on page 5

"Time Block/Methods Matrix " on page 7

"Navigating the Training Plans " on page 8

"Understanding the Icons " on page 9.

Sourcebook Organization

Here is a rundown on the chapters in this sourcebook, each devoted to a single topic. They are:

1 **"Introduction" starts on page 1**

A quick look at how the sourcebook works, and where to go for components you might need.

2 **"Background" starts on page 11**

Provides the context for your leadership workshops. It discusses why leadership is important to organizations in the late twentieth century. It provides synopses of various writers views on the topic and spotlights *leadership* rather than *management* skills.

3 **"Workshop Preparation" starts on page 35**

Gives general tips on workshop preparation, including how to design, administer, facilitate, conduct, and follow up on the training program. The chapter also has a workshop agenda template, on which you can block out the flow of your workshop, and a comprehensive checklist to help you remember the myriad of details associated with planning and delivering a workshop.

4 **"One-Day Leadership Workshop" starts on page 59**

Offers a scripted training plan. The workshop is designed for team leaders, managers, or anyone whose role allows or would benefit from the practice of leadership. This workshop includes learning activities, skill-practice exercises, recommends assessment, and action planning, in addition to other typical learning activities in an active workshop setting.

5 **"Half-Day Leadership Workshop" starts on page 87**

Is a scripted half-day workshop on challenging the status quo and building vision. It is useful to both new and experienced managers and team leaders. It stresses the skill of listening openly and attentively and encourages participants to act on their insights. Skill practice and action planning encourage transfer of learning to the workplace.

6   **"One-Hour Leadership Workshop" starts on page 103**

A scripted interactive session on giving credit. It provides learners with the techniques, and insight into where and when to use the skill.

7   **"Participant Handouts" starts on page 109**

Here are the masters from which you can create participant handouts—ready to be reproduced as is, or customized to suit your needs. The handouts focus on the basics of leadership. They cover each of the major characteristics of leaders.

8   **"Learning Activities" starts on page 137**

Create the high level of participant involvement needed for learning. These activities run the gamut from visualization and role plays, to hands-on construction activities, brainstorming and introspective discussions.

9   **"Instruments and Assessments" starts on page 165**

This short collection includes self-appraisals; surveys in which participants identify their own performance in a number of key leadership practices. Some of these assessments may be run in a 360 degree mode. In such instances, feedback is graphed to provide participants with a graphic depiction of their own assessment in contrast to that of others.

10   **"Overhead Transparencies" starts on page 189**

Photocopy these camera-ready masters on transparency film for professional-looking visuals to reinforce your presentations.

Appendix   **"Resources for Training Professionals" starts on page 201**

To learn more about leadership, refer to the books and periodicals cited in the selected bibliography. To acquire training products, contact the providers.

Glossary   **Starts on page 205**

Index   **Starts on page 207**

Workshop Building Blocks

This sourcebook provides a comprehensive set of tools to facilitate your leadership training efforts. In addition to using these materials as suggested in the three training designs (chapters four through six), we encourage you to select and modify them as appropriate to your situation.

The following pages provide subject/reference and time block/ methods matrices to help you select building blocks that fit your objectives.

Directions

To use the "Subject/Reference Matrix" starting on page 5, follow the steps below:

1 To locate sourcebook material on a specific topic, go to the topic column and find the row that lists the topic needed.

2 Refer to the cells in the selected row to find page references for information and materials on the topic. For example, to locate learning activities on your chosen topic go to row 2.

3 Also, refer to the Appendix, "Resources for Training Professionals" starting on page 201, for titles of films/videos that meet your requirements.

Subject/Reference Matrix

Topic	Background	Scripts	Handouts	Overheads	Learning Activities	Instruments and Assessments
Facilitation and Administration	"Introduction" pp 1–10 "Background" pp 11–31 "Preparation" pp 35–56	"One-Day Leadership Workshop" starting on page 59 "Half-Day Leadership Workshop" starting on page 87 "One-Hour Leadership Workshop" starting on page 103				The assessments "Leadership Assessment (Other)" on page 167, and "Listening Assessment (Other)" on page 174 may be used before the training to gather 360 data for participants.
Challenging the Status Quo	"Characteristic #1: Question Groupthink" p 19 "Characteristic #2: Reset Direction" pp 21–25	"Half-Day Leadership Workshop" pp 95–97	"Openness and Vision" pp 117–118 "Leaders Learn by Listening" p 120	"Build on Strengths" p 198	"I Think I Can" pp 157–158	"Paradigm Self-Assessment" pp 170–171 "Listening Self-Assessment" p 173 "Information Gathering Mode Assessment Guidelines" p 182
Leadership Characteristics	"What Is Leadership?" p 12 "Leadership Characteristics Chart" p 13 Creating Followership" pp 15–16 "Leadership Differences" pp 16–18	"One-Day Leadership Workshop" pp 68–69	"Leadership Characteristics" p 110 "A Leader I've Known" p 112 "Recognizing Leadership" p 113 "Types of Leaders" pp 115–116	"Leadership Characteristics" p 193	"Values Activity Guidelines" p 145 "It's Up to Us to Decide" pp 146–148	"Leadership Assessment Guidelines" pp 166–167 "Goal Setting Self-Assessment Guidelines" p 179

Subject/Reference Matrix

Topic	Background	Scripts	Handouts	Overheads	Learning Activities	Instruments and Assessments
Vision	"Characteristic #2: Reset Direction" pp 21–23 "What Does It 'Look' Like?" p 23 "Communicating the Vision" p 23 "Power of Vision Statements" p 25	"One-Day Leadership Workshop" pp 71–72 "Half-Day Leadership Workshop" pp 98–102	"Openness and Vision" p 117 "How Vision Develops" p 121 "How to Communicate Vision" pp 123–124	"Vision Defined" p 196 "Communicate the Vision" p 187	"Which One Is a Vision?" pp 150 "Images Are Everywhere" pp 140–141 "A Few of My Favorite Things" pp 142–143 "Visualization Activity Guidelines" pp 154–155	"Listening Assessment Guidelines" p 172
Support Purposeful Action	"Characteristic #3: Guide Cooperative Actions" pp 25-27	"One-Day Leadership Workshop" pp 75–78	"Roles and Responsibilities" p 125 "Tailor Your Coaching" p 126 "Training the Team" p 128 "Autonomy and Control" p 129	"Build on Strengths" p 198 "Autonomy and Control" p 199	"I Think I Can" pp 157–158	"Coaching Assessment Questionnaire" p 177 "Giving Constructive Feedback" p 161
Role Model	"Characteristic #4: Walk the Talk" p 28	"One-Day Leadership Workshop" pp 79 -80			"You're Signaling" p 159	The 360 aspect of assessments
Provide Encouragement	"Characteristic #5: Motivate Others—Extrinsic Vs. Intrinsic Motivation" p 29	"One-Day Leadership Workshop" pp 82–85 "One-Hour Leadership Workshop" pp 103–112	"Intrinsic and Extrinsic Motivation" p 130 "Encouraging the Individual Team Member" p 131 "Giving Positive Feedback" p 132 "Opportunities to Celebrate Success" p 134	"Motivate the Team" p 200 "Giving Positive Feedback" p 194	"Giving Constructive Feedback" pp 160–161 "Giving Credit" pp 162-164	"Opportunities to Celebrate Success" pp 186-187

Time Block/Methods Matrix

Directions

If you have a limited time frame in which to introduce a skill, you may find the following suggestions helpful. To select a training method that fits a particular time block, locate in the first column the row that lists the time block you wish to fill. Any of these activities, particularly role plays and those involving discussions, can easily expand to an hour. If you use some of the videos suggested in the Appendix, your training session can expand to two or two-and-a-half hours.

Time Block Available	Learning Activities	Instruments and Assessments
30 minutes or less	Choose any one of the following: "Life Path" p 139 "Images Are Everywhere" p 141 "A Few of My Favorite Things" p 143 "It's Up to Us to Decide" pp 146–148 "Case One" p 146 "You're Signaling" p 159 "Giving Constructive Feedback" p 161 "Giving Credit" p 163	Choose any one of the following: "Paradigm Self-Assessment" p 171 "Information Gathering Mode Assessment Guidelines" p 182 "Leadership Assessment Guidelines" p 166 "Goal Setting Self-Assessment Guidelines" starting on p 179 "Listening Assessment Guidelines" p 172
30 minutes or longer	Combine any one of the learning activities with a handout and a self-assessment.	
2–3 hours	Combine an activity and an assessment on a single topic with one of the videos suggested in "Resources for Training Professionals" starting on page 201.	

Navigating the Training Plans

The training plans are the heart of the seminar and workshop sessions—the glue that draws and holds everything together. These training plans are set out in detail on a module-by-module basis, with an *agenda, statement of purpose,* and *objectives* for each module. We have attempted to make these training plans as easy to use and as complete as possible. A sample with annotations is shown on page 10. Look for the following elements in each training plan:

1   Each major portion within a module has a section heading and a statement of purpose for the section and suggested timing.

2   Within each section, one or more major activities, marked by an icon and a descriptive heading.

3   Additionally, you will find a number of supporting activities, each activity marked with an icon and explained with a suggested action.

4   Suggested actions are shown in conjunction with supporting activities, with the appropriate action verb in uppercase ***BOLD ITALICS***.

5   Suggested comments accompany many of the suggested actions. While these comments are fully "scripted," convert them to your own words. Keep the key thoughts, of course, but paraphrase in a way that is meaningful to you and participants.

6   There are also places for your notes to personalize the material to your group and your training style.

Understanding the Icons

Major activities   *These icons mark major activities:*

Activities that feature facilitator commentary. In these activities, you—as facilitator—present information that will be key to subsequent workshop activities.

Activities carried out in large group discussion. Such activities typically follow major exercises on which participants have worked individually or in groups.

Activities that revolve around table group discussion. This icon is also used as a signal to listen for specific comments.

Activities completed on an individual basis.

Support activities   *These icons indicate supporting activities:*

Display an overhead transparency. The text accompanying the icon references the transparency title.

Have group read, distribute a participant handout, part or all of a learning activity, or an assessment, or point something out.

Pose a question. Wording for the question follows, as do suggested answers, when appropriate.

Uncover a flipchart, or develop one, based on participant feedback.

Transition to another subject or activity.

Call attention to time.

Sample Page

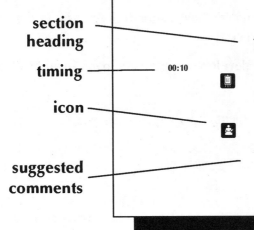

Leadership   Half-Day Leadership Workshop

Training Plan

Purpose   This workshop section establishes an environment in which
                     participants and facilitator are at ease with each other, and in which
                     participants have a clear understanding of what to expect and what
                     is required of them.

Objectives   On completion of this workshop segment, participants should be
                     able to:

   - View the workshop setting as one of active involvement.
   - Describe the flow and duration of the workshop.
   - Understand the expectations for participation in the session.
   - Identify the other participants in the session.
   - Know the importance of vision.
   - Define their personal objectives for the training session.

AGENDA: Introduction to the Workshop	Minutes 60	Start/Stop 8:00/9:00	Actual Start / Stop
"Welcome and Introductions " on page 91	10	8:00 / 8:10	
"Overview of the Workshop " on page 92	5	8:10 / 8:15	
"Agenda and Logistics " on page 92	5	8:15 / 8:20	
"Roles and Responsibilities " on page 93	10	8:20 / 8:30	
"Assessment" on page 93: fill out, score	30	8:30 / 9:00	

section heading ——

1 ... **Introduction to the Workshop (8:00 to 9:00)**

timing —— 00:10

icon ——

Welcome and Introductions

BEFORE participants arrive at the session, prepare a flipchart welcoming them and identifying the topic and length of this session. You also may develop a second flipchart that identifies the characteristics of the session environment.

WELCOME participants to the session and make these points:

suggested comments ——

   - This is a full half-day workshop which focuses on the most distinguishing characteristic of leaders—*their vision*.

91

Chapter Two:

Background

This Chapter

… covers the background of leadership training:

Why leadership is important in today's organizations, and what it is.

Many leadership topics are covered in these training materials. Since leadership encompasses many topics that deserve training focus in their own right, many of these not covered in this training—coaching, teamwork, quality, diversity, basic management skills—are dealt with in other volumes in this series.

Organization of the remainder of the book.

Why Leadership?

There is renewed interest in organization leadership. A few always felt it important. For a long time theirs were lonely voices—regarded by many as impractical, theoretical, idealistic. Emphasis was on management and training in skills involved in *planning, organizing, directing,* and *controlling.* These remain important, but it has become clear that these efforts are not enough.

Organization changes

Winning organizations—governments, businesses, nonprofit—need to embody more than efficient practices. The best organizations have an esprit de corps that infuses efficiency. It leads to enthusiasm, creativity and innovation, better quality, and more satisfied customers. Such organizations *listen* better—to customers, employees, stakeholders, and the communities where they do business. We call this difference *leadership.*

The need for leadership has become obvious. Organizations continue to down-size, removing layers of management. Technology has played a role in this, as has the need to improve productivity, efficiency, and profitability. Those who remain face change: more adaptability, less supervision, more worker-level responsibility for decisions about work processes and schedules. It has become evident that we need to empower workers, so they will take initiative and assume leadership roles without the authority of position.

Leaders must be adaptive and innovative. As the world economy becomes more global, organizations have to respond differently. There is greater competition, and it is more varied. Customers, workers, and other stakeholders represent different cultural viewpoints. These pressures have required greater openness, creativity, and innovation, greater attention to *quality* and *cost-effective practices*. Work practices must reflect this diversity.

It is evident there is need for leaders who can help people find meaning and commitment in the workplace. Those who have lost jobs in organizational restructuring have also changed. Many were high achievers who had "played the game," advancing through dedication and hard work. To have become redundant or replacable has led to a realization that there is a thing called *healthy self-interest*. Many have vowed never again to be so involved, or loyal. This is a great loss—to the workers themselves as well as the organizations they work with.

Abuse of power

The need for principled leaders has become clear. Reports of abuse of authority and power have grown. Financial institutions have failed to regulate themselves—often making not just unsound but unethical decisions. Investment scandals have mushroomed, demonstrating greed and lack of ethics. Organizations have been fined for unfair practices in soliciting business. Once the business is secure, many have been found to overcharge unfairly. The finest of our young have been caught in wholesale cheating. Elected officials have affronted the public with self-interested bickering, jockeying for position, or defending the status quo, rather than focusing on the public good. Many ask what has happened to principles like honesty, integrity, justice, loyalty, and morality.

What Is Leadership?

Most people feel they know what leadership is but have a hard time describing it. That is perfectly understandable! We know we understand *what* leadership is, because we recognize leaders when we see and hear them. That is because we *agree* with them or we *see* the appeal they have to followers. Perhaps they even *inspire* us. We want to follow. The presence of *followers* is an essential part of being a leader. You can't lead if no one is following!

Leadership Characteristics Chart

Kouzes & Posner *The Leadership Challenge*	Warren Bennis *Leaders, Why Leaders Can't Lead*	Ken Blanchard *Situational Leadership, The One-Minute Leader*	Terry Anderson *Transforming Leadership*	Tom Peters *Thriving on Chaos*	Stephen Covey *Principle-Centered Leadership*	John P. Kotter *A Force for Change*
Challenges the process	Creates an inspired vision	Sets clear goals	Well-defined sense of mission, purpose, values, goals	Vision that guides all activity	Continually learning	Establishing direction
Inspires a shared vision	Manages others by example	Provides clear directions	Exceptional physical health	Self-confident	Service oriented	Aligning people
Enables others to act	Visible to employees, customers, vendors	Supports people as they need it	Exercises self-mastery	Willing to share achievement	Radiates positive energy	Aligning people
Models the way	Listens attentively	Delegates and empowers as followers are ready to accept	Uses course correction	Displays caring	Has love, supported by faith and hope	Motivating and inspiring produces change
Encourages the heart	Delegates to the front line	Provides feedback on performance.	Is results oriented	Decisive	Is typically grateful	
	Builds a flatter organization	Is flexible	Manages change	Committed to employees and their projects	Sense of wonder about life	
	Assures essential training		Develops teams to accomplish results	Likes to be surrounded by highly competent people	Courage combined with emotional vulnerability	
					Search for truth and beauty	
					Caring, sharing, and forgiving	

Since no one can be a leader without *followers*, it is important to know how a leader develops them. He or she captures followers' hopes and dreams. The leader's vision gives them a voice. Followers are first attracted to the leader when the *vision* the leader articulates resonates in them. The vision may address wrongs they care about, and it may cast the possible solution in *worthy* or even *heroic* terms. Achieving this future that followers care about is seen as a noble pursuit. This vision conforms to the values of those who are attracted to it.

Followers may become attached to the leader at any phase of the mission. Some join when they hear about the vision. Their commitment may come while working with the leader on projects related to the vision. As a committed core of followers forms, it attracts more people.

The root of the word *lead* means "to go." The *shared vision* takes followers toward a desired destination. We think of leaders as *people with a mission or vision, pioneers, those who inspire and encourage*, often leading us to accomplish our personal best. They are motivated and stimulate. Usually they have *strongly held principles*, which guides their actions. Being goal-oriented and *principle-centered*, they are agile in adjusting tactics to accommodate unforeseen obstacles that block them. How they get to the goal is not as important as the goal itself.

Leadership Characteristics

The findings of several who have studied leaders and written about their distinctive characteristics are summarized in the chart "Leadership Characteristics Chart" on page 13. While emphases may vary— for example, on principle centeredness, action or people orientation—all of these descriptions have common themes—*openness to change, ability to visualize the future, be guided by it and communicate it powerfully to others, entrust the mission to others, display commitment through action*, and *encourage followers*.

Characteristic #1—Questioning groupthink by:
Being curious—investigating, asking "why," asking questions, listening, verifying understanding, reflecting, and

- Taking initiative, risks, experimenting

- Being open to diverse opinions

- Encouraging creativity, innovation

Characteristic #2—Resetting direction by:

Developing a vision—synthesizing recurring themes and values, and

- "Selling" the vision—presenting a compelling vision of a possible future

- Enlisting others—asking for help, showing how they can make a difference

Characteristic #3—Guiding cooperative actions by:

Planning, setting team goals, and

- Empowering *followers*

- Encouraging *initiative*

- Delegating *authority*

- Coaching, *monitoring*

- Providing *constructive feedback*

Characteristic #4—"Walking the talk" by:

Being involved—setting an example of personal commitment and

- Committing to quality outcomes

- Helping solve problems

- Being persistent

Characteristic #5—Motivating others by:

Recognizing individual and team contributions and

- Giving positive feedback

- Celebrating accomplishments

- Reinforcing teamwork

Creating Followership

By definition, to be a leader, you need followers. And followers need direction. The leader provides this direction by resetting the sights of the followers on a new vision and leading the way through personal action. Followers respond to the new vision because it captures some inner sense of rightness. Followers "join" the leader at all phases of an endeavor, in the early stages when a direction is being charted or later when many followers are already committed to making the vision become a reality through action.

Leaders demonstrate commitment to the vision *by example*. They are role models of personal involvement. They are persistent. They don't give up easily. Stress, frustration, even exhaustion does not deter them. They challenge others to do the same.

Leaders create an *appreciative climate*. It is true that many may resist the leader's challenge to the status quo. This may be negative faultfinding, ridicule, or even character assassination. However, the leader fosters the commitment of the followers by *continually reinforcing* the vision and providing *positive feedback*. When milestones are achieved leaders recognize accomplishments and individual contributions. They foster *cooperation* and *teamwork*. They *encourage collaboration* by stressing the common goal and recognizing team wins. They support team members by coaching, listening, paying attention to detail, giving credit for accomplishments, and helping in problem situations.

Leader's Source of Power

Many leaders are promoted to or voted into positions of power, where a certain level of "command" is bestowed on them as a result of that position. We call this *position power*, the legitimate power which comes with the position—to reward or coerce. People in the position can abuse this power.

In addition to position power, leaders rely heavily on *personal power*. This consists of the power followers freely bestow on a leader, because of the leader's vision, values, or personal characteristics. We call this *referent power*. In addition, a leader is often an *expert* in some area—either through interest or training. Such a leader can *train, coach,* and *mentor* others. Often, leaders are expert in communications, management, or motivational skills. Use of personal power is often preferable, even when a leader can demand, through power of position.

Leadership Differences

Fundamental to all leadership is the leader's own style. This can be described as *personality* type or *behavioral* style. Personality refers to underlying preferences, which like paradigms, color one's typical responses to others and one's environment. Behavior looks only at the patterns of action (habits) that one uses. Those who follow the former use a Myers-Briggs type assessment model (Katherine C. Briggs and Isabel Briggs Myers, *Myers-Briggs Type Indicator* [Palo Alto: Consulting Psychologists Press, Inc.]) while those who follow the latter may use a modified Merrill (four-quadrant) model (David W. Merrill, Ph.D., *Social Style* [Denver, The TRACOM Corporation]). The important thing to note about either one, is that:

- Leaders come in all personality and behavioral types.

- Understanding of personality types provides insight into oneself and others.

- Personality plays a major role in sending and receiving communications.

- While understanding styles legitimately falls within leadership training, it is not covered in this sourcebook. (Resources on this topic are mentioned below or listed in the Appendix.)

When we think of some of the characteristics of leaders it might appear that they are found only in very democratic environments. Or that all leaders espouse values that we admire. Or that the characteristics which seem so appealing in the abstract, are always admirable. Not so! History tells us that is not the case. Leaders come in all personality types and behavioral styles. They espouse a spectrum of values. They are found in all cultures. They are at once products of those environments and their architects. Writers describe these differences in leadership styles in different ways—after one set of ancient gods or another. Other writers describe them in more common cultural terms. The following, highly simplified, synopsis owes its genesis to these sources, Sandra Krebs Hirsh and Jean M. Kummerow,[1] William Schneider,[2] and Charles Handy.[3]

- *High-control* environments both attract and nurture leaders who are more inclined to be traditional, stabilizing forces. These leaders work from a strong sense of responsibility, loyalty, and industry. They tend to be excellent in environments that require disciplined processes and timely output. Such leaders are more controlling.

- *Highly challenging* or *volatile* environments attract and advance leaders with a bent for troubleshooting, negotiating, and firefighting. Such leaders may be bored by the routine but are challenged by the unexpected. Such leaders need to constantly "raise the bar." They are highly innovative.

- Environments that *value ideas* and *personal values* attract and develop leaders whose temperament is energized by introspection, breakthrough thinking, and interaction with people. Such leaders are moved by a personal sense of possibilities and a strong sense of mission. They are inspiring.

---

1. *Introduction to Type in Organizations*, 2nd edition, Palo Alto, Consulting Psychologist Press, Inc., 1990
2. *The Re-engineering Alternative: Making Your Corporate Culture Work for You*, New York, Irwin One, 1994
3. *Gods of Management: The Changing Work of Organizations*, London, Arrow Books, 1995

- *Entrepreneurial* environments attract and encourage leaders who have strong strategic senses. These leaders combine *creativity* and *ingenuity* with *logic*. They are *courageous* and *strategic*.

We are usually attracted to work environments that match our temperaments, just as we respond to leaders who are like ourselves.

Leaders Are Good Communicators

The skill of communicating effectively is also fundamental to all leadership competencies—asking questions with curiosity, listening to understand, and explaining ideas in a *compelling* and *forceful* way. The communications model that we use is the one that is used in other volumes of this series. These skills include those listed in the table below.

Leader Communications

Skill	Examples
Observing	• **Surroundings** such as physical environment, or behavioral equipment, that convey information about background, personality, etc.
	• **Personal Effects** such as grooming and clothing as they relate to a person's sense of self.
	• **Mood** indicators such as facial expressions, mannerisms, gestures.
Questioning	• **Open questions** beginning with who, what, why, how, and when—which invite longer than one word answers.
	• **Leading** questions which invite a specific and already known answer—typically thought to be manipulative.
	• **Implication** questions which ask the speaker to speculate on consequences and possibilities—what if, how might etc.
	• **Closed** questions which can easily be answered by a simple "yes" or "no."
Listening	• **Attending** to the speaker.
	• **Processing** what the speaker is saying or implying.
	• **Taking notes** as an aid to memory.
	• **Practicing** memory techniques.

Verifying	• **Rephrasing** what has been understood for the purpose of acknowledging the speaker, demonstrating listening and assuring understanding.
	• **Asking** the speaker to assure that he/she has been understood.
Explaining	• **Clear** and **concise** directions and instructions.
	• **Vivid descriptions** of events or possible future.
	• **Presentation** of the vision in vivid and compelling way.

The most effective leaders also have good *management skills.* They plan carefully, recognizing that the team can often help identify the best approaches. Most know that ownership by team members requires them to delegate, empower, focusing on outcomes rather than insisting on control of the process. If they are good people managers, or if their span of control is limited to where they know all the team members, they build on team strengths.

Characteristic #1:
Question Groupthink

When unsure how to behave, most people take their lead from what others are doing. This type of *social proof* tends to become an *automatic pilot* that directs the behavior of many. Many refer to this as *Groupthink.* Other inputs to this automatic pilot may be tradition, peer consensus, or the directives of authorities. All tend to provide direction within pre-set patterns. The trouble with such patterns is that they frequently outlive the conditions that gave rise to them. Or they may have been initially based on false assumptions.

The leader is most apt to question these habits. Kouzes and Posner refer to this as *challenging the process….* To those who have experienced faultfinders, the word *challenging* may have negative connotations. Others, who like life to be orderly and predictable, may find the tendency to constantly question unsettling. Questioning groupthink is the positive habit of questioning in a curious and open way. The result often is new and improved processes.

Curiosity

Leaders tend to be interested in all kinds of things. They ask a lot of questions, particularly "why." This is not motivated by a desire to find fault. Leaders are good listeners, because they are genuinely

19

interested in hearing what others have to say. They hear what customers and co-workers suggest or request. Customers request *product innovations.* Employees/volunteers suggest *work changes.*

They note *inconsistencies, inefficiencies,* and *unmet needs.* When input combines into a clear message a vision emerges. This insight is unique to the leader's point of view.

All leader insights are *not* valid. Many are not. When they reveal themselves as *unfeasible, improbable,* or *unworkable,* the leader discards them. It is important to know that the leader is not afraid to test insights and find them wanting. In early stages, they are as open to others' challenges as they are to their own. This open discussion helps them focus on the essentials of what is wrong with the current approach and why it should be changed, and what pursuing the vision could accomplish.

Initiative

Leaders test their ideas in action. Unlike dreamers, they test and refine. They don't see rejection of ideas as failure. They have a type of courage, an ability to maintain a positive outlook. This ability to handle failure, change, and stress is referred to as *resilience* or *psychological hardiness.*

This risk taking and willingness to let go of comfortable and familiar processes is a cornerstone of continuous work-process improvement in action. Leaders who focus on the essential goals, challenge those routines that stifle creativity and vitality.

Openness

Openness is consistent with innovation and checking the relevance of routines. Leaders are more apt to "think outside the box" (referring to the solution to the nine-dot puzzle whose dots are connected by four straight lines), to try new and unproved methods to achieve goals. They champion team efforts to cut *steps, time,* or *effort* from a function.

Paradigm awareness

The great enemy of openness is not an unwillingness to see things from the viewpoint of others, but the *inability* to do so. Joel Barker calls this *paradigm blindness,* which he describes as the tendency to perceive what we expect, the inability to notice or take seriously phenomena outside our expectations. He cites examples of inventions—xerography, the quartz watch—which ran counter to conventional methods and were ignored or rejected by those to whom they were shown.

Overgeneralizing

Overgeneralizing is a cause of paradigm blindness. One of the great learning advantages humans have is the ability to generalize. We intuit a rule from several examples and apply that rule to all instances of that class. This ability to generalize—to organize experience, to see patterns, relationships, underlying laws—helps us integrate new knowledge and is an essential trait of leaders when developing vision.

A rule can be over-applied, however. We call that *over-generalizing*. We all do this at times—fail to realize that a rule which applies *most* of the time has *exceptions*, or that there are other generalizations which are equally valid, even if we do not yet know them. We sometimes refer to overgeneralizing as *stereotyping* or the result as having a *mindset*. Both connote closed and unfair mindedness. Overgeneralizing is damaging when it leads to categorizing people or ideas. It leads us to disregard unique traits.

Fear

Another opponent of openness is fear. Most of us fear some unknown. That fear is the basis of predicting the dire consequences of change—eventualities which include the loss of cherished values, economic effects, or inability to learn new ways of doing things.

Characteristic #2: **Reset Direction**

Leaders develop a vision which guides them. There is nothing mystical about vision. Neither is it commonplace. It is not the result of analytical thought alone—it also requires insight and intuition. The word vision connotes

- A vivid image.

- An ideal or standard of excellence.

- A future orientation or desired destination.

What is a vision?

Instead of *vision*, many prefer to use other words—such as *goal, mission, objective, calling,* or *personal agenda*. Whatever the name, vision is a vivid picture of both a *future destination* and the *journey along the way*. It is rich in detail and feeling. You know what it will look or sound like, how it will feel, and what it will be like when you reach the destination. This image provides *focus* and *context* for a leader's or his/her followers' efforts. Such vision is consistent with the larger context of their lives—their *values, personal strengths, experiences,* and—within organizations—its *overall mission* or *overriding challenge*.

Developing a vision

One must use creativity to develop this image. Many of us left this part of ourselves in kindergarten—or want everyone to think we did. But anyone can create a vision.

To develop a vision, we must become immersed with the topic or problem so the mind is thoroughly engaged. This means that we develop visions about things with which we are already engaged. That engagement must be mental as well as physical. The vision may start with a persistent problem or with formal planning activities with which we break the project into components, and put time frames to them. Or it might start with reading or discussion.

Once the mind is engaged with the prospect, it starts to develop scenarios. Small snatches of what might happen become vivid images. John Robinson, in his book *Coach to Coach,* details this process. He likens it to the daydreaming all are familiar with since childhood. He also points out that the imagination becomes active when the leader pulls back from hands-on activities in what he describes as *30-second sabbaticals.*

This *vivid image* packs a great amount of information. The image is useful as the leader journeys toward the goal, tests possible scenarios against it, and answers questions by consulting it.

How to start a vision

Everyone's personal vision for the future derives from

- Past experiences.

- Personal values.

- Listening to others—co-workers, customers, suppliers.

- Reflection—one's own intuition, ability to make connections to generalize.

Visions start vaguely. If visions are to grow, we become more attached to them as they develop.

Visions grow when shared

The way to clarify a vision is to discuss it with others—*friends, co-workers, anyone* who will listen. What started as a vague notion will either become more vivid and compelling, or it will fizzle out. It's as if discussing it and acting on it brings the distant image closer and makes it more focused.

Influence of experiences

To build a vision we use our organizational and industry experience, as well as our past accomplishments and mistakes. By first looking at our past, experts indicate that we develop a longer time horizon and richer detail when envisioning the future. The more varied the experience and the input we've gathered, the more possibilities we see in current situations.

Why visions attract

Experience, desire, reflection, imagination, insight, and intuition combine forces. The result is a unique spin on a current situation that challenges by asking "why not?" The vision is known to be possible. This challenge to action is a defining characteristic of visions, separating them from dreams. In challenging others to achieve the possible, leaders show others how attractive the future could be. This view resonates with followers because it often reflects their input, and often articulates their own views and secret desires.

What does it "look" like?

Each person's *vision* is defined in terms that are meaningful to him or her. Some imagine images; others hear reactions or imagine their feelings when the goal is achieved. Some people "see" their vision; others "hear" it or imagine it unfolding like a play. Thinking about it, talking about it and taking action on it helps make it more vivid. This vividness develops over time. It is supported by desire that may come from a wish to help others, a large ego, or because it seems the right thing to do. In other words, it reflects the leader's own values.

Communicating the vision

Once the vision is vividly perceived, the leader must be able to communicate it. Leaders feel the need to communicate their vision because they *strongly believe in* and are *compelled to act on it*. To communicate it effectively, the leader must be able to *present* ideas effectively.

Prepare a vision statement

Here are some pointers for preparing a compelling vision presentation:

1 Write a *clear, concise* statement of your vision. It should be possible to present it in five minutes or less. Check it for logical development, clarity, and simplicity.

2 Find *examples* that illustrate the *central point*. These may be heroic, such as a well-known historic event; local, such as an event all are familiar with; or a human interest example that appeals to the heart. Integrate these illustrations into the message.

3 Create a *metaphor* (or two) that serves to illustrate what you are talking about. This should be something that people can relate to and that helps you make your point *vividly* or *humorously*.

4 Identify a *key phrase*. Is there a key phrase that you might use as a refrain? Is there a line of poetry, a line from a song, hymn, or historic document that resonates with the idea you are describing? Integrate quotations and key phrases into your presentation.

5 *Practice* the presentation and adjust it to the point where you are comfortable with it. Comfort is being able to convey your

　　　　　　　　　　　　　desired feeling while you escape the tension of speaking.

Example　　　　　　Listen to Martin Luther King's "I Have a Dream" speech. It models all the elements of a well constructed vision statement and conveys the emotional intensity that a truly held vision statement conveys. It clearly resonates with his audience as a reflection of their own dreams. It has:

Characteristic	Example
Refrain	"I have a dream… " "Free at last"
Central message	All people will enjoy the same freedoms, no matter what skin color
Images	Mountains, red clay, little white and black children, heat
Figures of speech	Let freedom ring
Echoes historic language	*Bill of Rights* and *Bible*

Recite vision repeatedly　　　Once communicated, the leader never lets the team forget. John Kotter cites *under-communication* of the vision as a key factor for why some visions fail. The leader who reinforces the message, uses every available vehicle to do so! Some possibilities include:

- Review the message during frequent pep talks.

- Use phrases as *slogans* for activities, contests, etc.

- Refer back to it during *meetings* and *recognition* events.

- Place team members' roles in the context of *attaining the vision* when discussing their areas of responsibility.

- Tie it to the overall goal of the organization.

- Make posters illustrating key phrases and *post* them in prominent places.

- Make medallions, coins, or plaques that remind individuals of their importance in a larger context.

- Use a key phrase as the name of a *newsletter* or other internal communication device.

- Write *editorials* on key aspects of the vision.

- Recognize and reward *behavior* that furthers the vision.

Power of vision statements　　　Sensory images and word associations affect our actions more than most of us believe. The smell of coffee may make you want the brew. The thought of items on a "to do list" may keep us from sleeping at night. At the end of the work day, the image of friends or family may lead some to leave hastily and shortchange an end-of-the-day-routine. The image of a customer's imagined smile in response to a call may encourage a salesperson to pick up the phone.

Athletes tell us that they imagine over and over again making winning plays, perfect shots, and winning the game. Their imagination is a mental rehearsal of the actions required, as well as a reinforcement of the desire to win. This is how leaders use images to reinforce their ability to reach goals.

Keep focus on the vision

Leaders need good management skills—planning, scheduling, communicating—to involve people in attaining the vision. Management skills are just the beginning, however. The leader does not develop work plans in isolation. Rather, he or she involves contributors in the process, since they are the experts in what works and what does not. Leaders recognize that those doing the work have more insight into how to plan or adjust the work process. The leader argues forcefully for adopting their suggestions to change processes. The leader considers several options and is open to novel ways of staffing to achieve desired outcomes.

Leaders also encourage contributors to set standards of performance that they can monitor. The leader monitors progress—not just in the usual way of checking progress on a regular basis, but through ongoing involvement and assistance.

Characteristic #3:
Guide Cooperative Actions

Leaders build cohesive teams, where each plays a role in a common mission. Both leaders and followers are on the same team. The leader demonstrates trust in the judgments and the decisions of the team—both when their ideas work and when they don't. The leader focuses on outcomes and competencies. The team is asked to help devise ways to achieve the quality, quantity, time frames, and service levels needed to achieve the goal. The leader requires the same openness to change and willingness to speak up from the team members. Leaders don't let problems linger. They involve the team in diagnosing what went wrong and correcting it. They value opinions, support risk taking, champion ideas of the team, and rely on co-workers to come through in their areas of responsibility.

Challenge people to be their best

Leaders give the example of performing at their personal best, and they *inspire* others to do the same. They challenge people to drop preconceptions that limit performance. Also, they show people they have capabilities they were unaware of and encourage them to trust and develop their talents.

They test the limits of their own abilities, talents, skills, and expertise. Optimistically they believe they can influence outcomes. They find challenging tasks meaningful and stimulating rather than stressful.

Empower/ encourage initiative

Leaders develop the habit of leadership within their teams by encouraging team members to make up their own minds about situations, and by encouraging people to act on their own insights, without having to seek prior approval. This benefits the entire team by allowing it to tap into the creativity and insight of all the team members, not just a designated few. It also develops the ownership of each team member in the team. This increased insight, perspective, involvement, and ownership adds to the entire team's ability to achieve results. Developing an empowered team, where each member acknowledges the right to think for himself, to take initiative, and, take responsibility for the outcomes of his actions is best supported by a leader who:

- Asks people doing the work their opinions.

- Treats ideas seriously, never ridiculing them.

- Teaches team members how to project the impact of their ideas in terms of costs and results.

- Gives people credit when their ideas lead to successful outcomes.

- When ideas lead to disappointing results, coaches team members to learn from them.

- Encourages a climate of trial-and-error, or successive approximations of an ideal.

- Allows people to make mistakes and teaches them how to learn from mistakes.

- Encourages team members to share what they have learned by trial-and-error.

- Solicits ideas on an ongoing basis. Formally acknowledges them. In some way rewards ideas that result in quality improvements or cost reductions—presentation to peers, cash bonuses, etc.

Delegate

Delegation is a prerequisite of the empowered team. In delegating, the leader needs to:

- Formally acknowledge the intent to delegate.

- Identify the scope of what is being delegated.

- Identify the circumstances and expectations surrounding this delegation—is the candidate to exercise the delegated authority only under certain circumstances, such as the absence of a leader? What are the reporting expectations: log of decisions, progress reports, etc.?

- Accurately assess the critical skills needed to successfully exercise the delegated authority.

- Provide training in critical skills.

- Provide coaching in exercising the delegated responsibility.

- Create an approachable environment, so that the person may seek advice or problem-solving assistance.

- Resist "taking back" the delegated responsibility, or telling people what to do.

- Provide encouragement to the person assuming the responsibility—positive feedback, support, hold up a yardstick of accomplishments.

Coach

Coaching, like delegation and autonomy, is an extensive topic in itself (See *Coaching* by Dennis Kinlaw in the ASTD Trainer's Sourcebook series.) Other useful books are also available on the topic. The leader is a coach in the sense that she/he seeks to guide performance by providing on-the-job support, based on the team members' own skills, the requirements of the task, and the vision.

Coaching interactions are tailored to the needs of the individual, based on his or her performance. Usually, coaching differs from training in that some of the requisite skills are present, and tips on refining the skills are given by the coach. Coaching may involve:

- Specific verbal feedback on the person's use of the skill.

- Specific attention to the technique or techniques which might be improved.

- Demonstration of a technique.

- Contrast of the "right" and "wrong" way to perform a technique.

- Role play or other practice.

Coaches tend to keep score, to note progress in the technique, and to correlate it to results.

Characteristic #4:
Walk the Talk

Leaders set example

Talking about the vision is not enough. Leaders must show enthusiasm through their own actions. Acting in conformity with the vision reinforces the group's sense of direction and serves as the best possible reinforcement. It also provides a model others can follow.

Followers of leaders can trust the integrity of those who act in conformity with the convictions they preach.

Acting consistently with their values and goals means:

- Being involved at every step of the way.

- Working long hours side-by-side with their team to accomplish their goals.

- Taking risks when there are no clear guidelines or when innovation is called for.

- Persisting, in spite of temporary setbacks.

- Monitoring progress and taking corrective action.

Team members also value the competence of the leader. They need to believe that the leader knows what he or she is doing. Belief in leader competence comes in large part from the evidence of the leader's track record. When a leader first emerges, judgment is reserved. As situations arise that require a leader's competence, judgments form. At lower levels, the required competencies tend to be more technical.

Characteristic #5: Motivate Others—
Extrinsic Vs. Intrinsic Motivation

One way of looking at motivation is to look at *intrinsic* versus *extrinsic* motivation.

Intrinsic rewards

A task is intrinsically motivating when it provides its own reward. The act of finishing a long or difficult process is often the moment of greatest satisfaction, even though there may not be recognition by others. A writer who finishes a long manuscript, a salesperson who has achieved acceptance of a proposal after a long sales cycle, a craftsman who finishes an intricate piece of work, all experience a thrill in executing their craft skillfully. We call this *intrinsic* motivation. Such tasks tend to be repeated.

You've often heard people say, "I can't believe that people pay me for doing this. I'm having so much fun." They have discovered the intrinsic reward in what they do. This is why it is important for leaders to learn how people like to work and to provide the preferred level of coaching or independence.

Extrinsic rewards

People are also motivated to do things by others. This is the *extrinsic* reward. It may be the recognition that results from completing tasks that are significant to others. The publication of the finished book and positive book reviews are extrinsic rewards to the writer. Recognition events for achieving milestones are extrinsic motivation to workers on long projects.

Extrinsic rewards are important to workers. They can take many forms:

- A public thank you
- Monetary incentives
- Plaques, or
- Special parking spaces

It is wise to keep extrinsic rewards simple, so that they do not overshadow or displace the intrinsic reward a person gets from doing the task.

Encouraging the Individual Team Member

Leaders know their people. This involves knowing what motivates each of them, how they like to work, and their skill and confidence levels. In addition, leaders like their people. Often, they refer to followers as family. They are involved and in touch with them.

They know their aspirations and dreams. They create ways to foster openness and to get to know people on a personal level.

Respect individuality

Fundamental to the bond that grows between leaders and individual contributors is a basic respect for individual and cultural differences. Cultural diversity presents many possible barriers to close relationships. People from different cultures respond to stress, time, and emotions in different ways. They also have different attitudes toward family, holidays, and ethical or religious values. They celebrate in different ways and enjoy different foods and music. To get beyond these barriers, a leader must have a genuine interest in learning how others live their lives, how they think about their families and jobs, and what they value.

Credit

Credit is one of the most powerful extrinsic motivators. In crediting individual performance, leaders must be careful to be *credible*. A credible source is one who demonstrates a *knowledge* of the specifics of an event and can describe the *significance* of the event in the context of a larger picture. Credit should also be given for effort and risk taking—even when they do not produce the desired results. Credit at such times should be coupled with constructive feedback and support in problem solving. This support involves teaching team members how to analyze failures (before the memory fades) to learn valuable lessons. The leader publicly credits team members when the opportunity arises.

Give credit

Giving credit is one of the most powerful, the easiest, and the most overlooked means of motivating people. No matter how autonomous or empowered the worker, everyone likes to know that what he or she is doing is being noticed and appreciated by someone. When giving credit:

1 Identify the result the person achieved.

2 Tell why that result was important to the mission.

3 State one or two elements about the behavior that were critical to achieving the result.

4 Express your appreciation.

There are reasons for each step. The first step acknowledges the person's performance and clearly signals your awareness. The second step ties the performance to the group's goal or mission. So far any paper-pusher could cope; next comes the really important part (third), in which the leader who is "out and about" among his group has no problem. Number three establishes credibility. It requires that you know what the person did, the risk he or she took, the effort required, the problems encountered—the real details. Finally, comes the "thank you."

Leaders are generous with credible crediting!

Credit Effort and Risk Taking

Leaders tend to focus on results. Yet people often make huge efforts, particularly when trying new processes or technology, possibly with disappointing results. Something goes wrong. Unforeseen problems arise. Outcomes or timeliness do not go as planned. These experiences, are important to the results-oriented team leader. How the leader responds determines how much *creativity, innovation,* or *risk* his or her team will be willing to take in the future.

Reinforcing risk taking, innovation, and honest effort that fails is as important as reinforcing the efforts that end in the desired results. From a motivation standpoint, successful workers derive intrinsic rewards from the task. On the other hand, the failed effort may be intrinsically punishing. The sensitive and involved team leader will not fail to credit workers for such efforts. In addition to crediting the risk taking or innovation effort, the leader joins workers in trying to identify the lessons learned from unfruitful efforts.

Create Team Environment

We is a telltale word for the leader. Leaders plan with the team. Team members own the process. By tapping into the leadership qualities in the team, the leader creates an atmosphere of *appropriate challenge, recognition for achievement,* and *support for risk taking.* Team members are challenged to use judgment, to take calculated risks, and even to make their own missteps. In a nurturing team environment, mistakes are a natural outcome of making decisions. It is important to learn from miscues and to correct them quickly. The effective leader provides the environment that nurtures this type of involvement and ownership.

Motivational theories that help us understand why people feel *rewarded* rather than *stressed* by challenging tasks, follow.

Set, maintain standards

Leaders know that high expectations are motivating. They also know that there is nothing more de-motivating than one or two team members who bring down the level or results for the whole team. Usually, team members will monitor from within. However, it is a leader's responsibility—to offer constructive feedback, as needed—in addition to ongoing training and coaching.

To give constructive feedback, the leader:

1   Makes a direct statement indicating what the *behavior or performance level* is and why it's a problem.

2   Asks the person to comment on what is *causing* this problem.

3   Discusses (back and forth) the consequences of the behavior or of the performance level continuing at its current level.

4   Asks the person to identify what he or she can do to improve the situation. Sets expected performance levels and time frames.

5   Agrees to next steps and a review date.

Performance levels are a requirement of membership on a team. All are responsible for maintaining them.

Celebrate milestones

Celebrating small successes is important, particularly early in a group effort where little progress is evident. Leaders constantly hold up *before* and *after* images for the team—so that they can recognize the progress made and take satisfaction and reinforcement from it. Some ideas people use are:

• *Before* and *after* photographs.

• PERT charts and time lines, with W*e Are Here!* stickers.

• Small awards—coffee mugs or some emblem that denotes the first steps taken.

• Graphic representations—steps, thermometers, scales, mountains, etc.—to depict progress toward the goal.

• Parties to celebrate accomplishments.

• Notices in newsletters, on bulletin boards, etc.

Build camaraderie

Some leaders have institutionalized occasions to credit team efforts and build team bonds. These include:

• Friday afternoon beer bashes, such as those favored by some Silicon Valley companies.

• Rankless gatherings such as the weekly *holy hour* practiced in some of the British armed forces. Here anybody can say anything that is on his or her mind to any other member of the fraternity, regardless of rank. Such fluid lines of communication evaporate after holy hour.

• Casual days—casual dress as a metaphor for the lifting of other communications barriers.

- Organization recreational events such as picnics, outings, sports teams.

- Organizational recognition celebrations and roasts.

- Organization-sponsored community service events including weekend clean-up projects, sponsorship of school or sporting events.

These activities tend to raise spirits and lower inhibitions, foster closeness, camaraderie, and trust.

Notes:

_____

_____

_____

_____

_____

_____

_____

_____

_____

_____

_____

_____

_____

_____

_____

Chapter Three:

Workshop Preparation

Workshops which appear to flow effortlessly are almost always the result of thorough preparation and careful attention to details.

This Chapter

... provides general tips on how to prepare for your leadership workshop, including:

"Designing Your Own Training Program " on page 36

"Getting Ready" on page 41

"Preparation Checklist " on page 45

"Workshop Agenda Template " on page 47

"Facilitator Preparation " on page 51

"Conducting the Workshop " on page 51

The tools in this chapter are designed to help you block out the flow of your workshop and remember the myriad of details associated with planning and delivering a highly energized and successful leadership training session.

Designing Your Own Training Program

To design your training program, you must *define client needs, determine program content, media,* and *select methods*.

Defining Client Needs

The factors below define the parameters within which you must design your workshop.

1   Participants' training needs.

Workshop content must meet participants' training needs. Ideally, needs are determined through an assessment process where actual employee knowledge and skills are compared with industry standards or other criteria. If deficiencies or needs are discovered, and if training can remedy the situation, then the enterprise arranges for the necessary training.

2   Time available for training.

Leadership is a broad topic. You could dip into one aspect in sixty minutes, give a one-day overview, or build a wide range of skills through a forty-hour program. Program length generally depends upon how long participants can be away from the job, as well as training costs.

3   Training budget.

The training budget will have a significant impact on the program length, number of trainees, training site, materials, equipment, and type of media used.

4   Group size and composition.

Group size and composition will influence your choice of instructional methods, media, and content. If you plan small group discussions and skill practice, limit the class to between fifteen and twenty four people. The larger or more participative the group, the longer it will take to cover each topic. The smaller or more reserved the group, the more quickly the workshop will move.

Determining Program Content

Once you know the participants' training needs, the length of the program, your budget, and the size and composition of the group, you are ready to select the workshop content. In conjunction with your client, you must decide:

- The content which meets the client's training objectives within the time and budget available.

- The activity level which is suitable for the group size and composition.

- How to sequence the information. Study Chapters 2 and 7 to help you select programmed sequence content. Break the workshop topics into teachable components or units that proceed from simple to complex, known to unknown. Use participant's existing knowledge base as your point of departure and build on that platform as you introduce new material. Also, relate the content to what participants do on the job.

Selecting Training Methods and Media

Once you've determined the workshop content and presentation sequence, you will be ready to select training methods and media. Methods are the techniques you use to teach the concepts and skills. Media are materials that illustrate the ideas being presented. Training methods and media must support the training objectives, fit the time block available, and be appropriate to the size and composition of the group. Training methods and media descriptions follow.

Training Methods

The methods listed below are employed in the one-day, half-day, and one-hour training agendas contained in this sourcebook.

Facilitator commentary

Your commentaries as the facilitator are the threads that hold the workshop together. Use commentaries of up to ten minutes to present key concepts, background information, or to summarize learning activities. When you give a commentary, follow the instructor adage: Tell them what you're going to tell them; tell them; and tell them what you told them.

Keep your commentaries lively by interspersing questions and answers. Alternate commentaries with exercises that require participants to apply knowledge or practice a skill. To make your material captivating and memorable, use humor, personal anecdotes, and relevant examples.

Give commentaries of between one and five minutes to bridge between one training method and another. For instance, if you have just completed small group discussions and are about to begin a skill practice, your commentary could summarize the learning gained during the small group discussions and introduce the skill practice.

Question, answer

The question and answer technique draws out the group's knowledge, keeps participants alert, creates involvement, and allows the facilitator to verify participants' understanding.

Individual activities

Individual activities include readings, written exercises, self-assessments, and action planning. Individual activities allow participants to work at their own pace and on their own agendas. Some people will complete their work more quickly than others. Have a supplemental assignment ready for early finishers.

Small group discussions, reports

Small group discussions involve participants and allow them to apply what they have learned. Discussions also give shy members a safe forum for contributing ideas. This method assigns participants to groups of two to six people with an assigned discussion topic. Ask them to create charts for posting, and tell them to be prepared to give a brief report to the class. Throughout the day, vary group composition so that participants will have the opportunity to work with different people.

Skill practice, feedback

Participants practice the concepts, skills, and techniques presented in the workshop and receive feedback from other participants and from the facilitator in structured role plays. Shy or reserved individuals sometimes resist skill practice. If you have a group that you think will be reticent about participating in a skill practice, use discussion cases or a front-of-room demonstration to introduce the activity.

Demonstrations

Give two participants a scenario involving a leader and a team member, and ask them to demonstrate the interaction. The success of a demonstration depends heavily on skill levels of individuals giving the demonstration; so, carefully select participants. You may wish to play a role in these demonstrations.

Self-assessments

Self-assessments are individual activities that allow participants to evaluate their use of certain behaviors. The results reveal strengths and areas for development, as well as provide the participant with a baseline against which to measure change.

Action planning

Participants plan to apply their new skills when they return to the workplace. They will do this by setting developmental goals and implementation dates.

Instructional media

The media listed below are recommended for use in conjunction with the workshops described in this sourcebook.

Overhead transparencies

Overhead transparencies help the *audience* and *you*. Participants find it easier to follow your presentation, and the visuals structure your remarks. Keep transparencies simple—no more than five lines horizontal format, seven lines vertical. Use a clean, solid 24-point typeface that reads easily from the back of the room.

Charts

You don't need artistic and lettering skills to use flipcharts to enliven presentations and record group discussions. Display them on an easel and then post them on a wall as a record of what has been covered. Facilitators with poor lettering skills can call on participant volunteers to record discussions. Charts are excellent for recording information generated during the workshop. Make sure everyone can see them.

Printed handouts

Handouts give participants pertinent reference material and minimize the need for note taking. To facilitate distribution and use, put all your handouts (except those where you want an element of surprise) in a packet with numbered pages, and pass it out at the beginning of the workshop. In addition to receiving detailed reference material, participants also appreciate having copies of your overhead transparencies. You can reduce these and present them 2- or 4-up on the page.

Videos/films

Videos and films are options for presenting concepts, illustrating how concepts apply, dramatizing interactions, and showing positive behavior models. Through video, participants can learn from experts who might not be available in person, either because of their schedule, death, or your training budget.

Generally, show only one video per half-day of session. Possible exceptions include five-minute or less session openers or closers. Also, stop-and-go videos that are designed to be viewed in short segments followed by discussion and/or skill practice. Never show a film or video immediately after lunch, unless it is a spellbinder or uproariously funny.

Keep Spotlight Moving

To keep energy and interest levels high, vary your methods and media. In an effective training program, the spotlight moves around the room. During facilitator commentaries, the eyes are on the trainer. During a demonstration, one or two participants share attention. When people serve as small group spokesperson, they have center stage.

Those who actively participate learn best. If you try to carry the entire workshop load, you'll end up with a raspy throat, sore feet, and drowsy participants. Turn the spotlight around the room and you'll have enthusiastic, active learners. Equally important, you'll maintain the high energy level required to be at your best for the entire workshop.

Getting Ready

There are a number of administrative functions to perform prior to and after the workshop. Experienced facilitators find the best way to keep track of all the details is with checklists similar to those that follow on the next two pages. While you may not want every item on the list for every workshop, you can use this list as a starting point to develop a personalized version that exactly suits your needs.

You don't have to perform all these functions yourself. Often an administrative support person on the employee training and development staff can take responsibility for many administrative tasks. Likewise, if the meeting is being held at a hotel or conference center, a member of the sales and catering staff can oversee room, food service, and audiovisual equipment arrangements. Of course, you will still need close coordination and diligent follow-up to ensure success.

Use a copy of "Workshop Agenda Template" on page 47 to block out your programs and to plan what training methods and media best suits your training objectives.

Announce the Session

It is wise to enlist the support of an executive in the organization for the session. This support can take on one of a number of forms, such as the following:

1   Send out the invitations under the executive's signature.

Draft a letter such as the following for the executive's signature. Produce the copies for his/her signature. Make sure it goes out three to four weeks before the session.

Executive Endorsement

Dear _____,

For organizations such as ours, leadership is a crucial issue. Organizations can be most successful when they have enlisted the hearts and ingenuity of all their workers. Your insights can help us improve our processes, products, the work atmosphere, even the work experience.

With this in mind, we are sponsoring a series of leadership sessions. These will be held on the following schedule [list dates]. I am happy to invite you to attend the one on [date]. Please call [name of contact] at [phone number] and advise us of your availability.

Because this topic is important to all of us, I want to advise that you cannot accommodate other appointments on the day you attend a session. Your time for telephone calls will also be limited. It is advisable, therefore, to clear your calendar for the day. If this requires you to delegate responsibilities in order to devote full attention to the session, please do so.

I believe we all need this training and that the investment our organization is making in it will produce valuable returns.

Sincerely,

[name of executive]

Newsletter Announcement

Leadership Training Scheduled

I'm proud to announce that [organization name] has scheduled a series of leadership workshops which will be open to all employees [name the levels]. These sessions are being conducted by [facilitator name(s)] over the next several months.

Leadership at all levels is critical for the continued growth and innovation required in our competitive environment [use your own words to describe your environment]. It is through our combined dedication to our organization's goals and the creativity and insight of our employees on every level, that we will continue to refine our processes and services [or products] and lead our industry in market share [or whatever is appropriate]. [Organization name] is well aware that it is the creativity, ingenuity, and dedication of our workers that makes us what we are today.

As a means of renewing our commitment to excellence, I encourage all of you to take this opportunity to renew your leadership skills and to share with your colleagues.

2   Draft a copy of an endorsement of the session to appear in the organization's newsletter under the executive's name.

3   Invite the executive to attend lunch with the attendees.

4   Invite the executive to hand out certificates of completion at the end of the session.

Certificate of Completion

Before the session, duplicate and personalize certificates such as the "Certificate of Achievement" on page 56. You or the executive should hand them out at the end of the session.

Prepare for the Session

Preparing for a leadership training session requires a planning period for what you are going to train and then a recurring administrative preparation for each session.

Participant Roster

Include all the information you're going to need. You will probably create this on computer. See the reproducible form, "Participant Roster Worksheet" on page 48.

A sample participant roster follows. Record enrollment requests on a photocopy of this sheet, or create a virtual form in your computer. When the list is finalized, sort it alphabetically and print a copy to use as a workshop sign-in sheet. To prepare a *name tent* and *certificate of achievement* for each participant, use the reproducible masters on pages 57 and 56, respectively.

Planning Your Training Session

Agenda
- ☐ Plan the dates.
- ☐ Finalize the agenda.
- ☐ Identify timeframes, times for breaks, lunch, etc.
- ☐ Send out session announcement and pre-work, if any.

Facilities
- ☐ Select room large enough for number of attendees.
- ☐ Order flipcharts, overhead, markers, etc.
- ☐ Indicate desired room set-up.
- ☐ Order refreshments, lunch, etc.
- ☐ Complete enrollment, scoring of pre-work, etc.

Participant materials
- ☐ Select handouts, activities, and assessments to be used in session.
- ☐ Send for duplication and binding.
- ☐ Arrange for delivery to training site.
- ☐ Have a supply of tent cards or name tags.
- ☐ Place notepads, pencils, markers, on every table.

Facilitator materials
- ☐ Copy facilitator notes.
- ☐ Copy facilitator notes for selected activities and assessments.
- ☐ Arrange facilitator notes in binder with tabs.
- ☐ Create overhead transparencies using masters.
- ☐ Mount overhead transparencies.

Flipcharts
- ☐ Create initial flipcharts.
- ☐ Create headings for anticipated flipcharts.
- ☐ Make sure there is enough paper and enough markers.

Refreshments
- ☐ Order refreshments for breaks and lunch.
- ☐ Make sure payment arrangements are verified.

Room setup
- ☐ Send map of desired setup to facilities management.

Preparation Checklist

Program title _____

Program date _____ Time _____

Name of facilitator _____

Location _____

Number of participants _____

Administration

- ☐ Schedule meeting site
- ☐ Determine furniture arrangement
- ☐ Determine food and beverage service
- ☐ Determine access time and method
- ☐ Distribute workshop announcements
- ☐ Send participant confirmations

Participant Materials

- ☐ Name tags or tent cards
- ☐ Handouts
- ☐ Copies of 1-page facilitator's biography
- ☐ Pens or pencils
- ☐ Ruled paper
- ☐ Evaluations
- ☐ Hard candy or mints
- ☐ Prizes

Trainer Materials

- ☐ Workshop agenda
- ☐ Training plan
- ☐ Overhead transparencies
- ☐ Videos/films
- ☐ 2x3 foot chart pads
- ☐ Hand-lettered charts
- ☐ Felt-tipped markers
- ☐ Transparency pens
- ☐ Masking tape
- ☐ Cellophane tape
- ☐ Dry-erase markers
- ☐ Chalk
- ☐ Erasers
- ☐ Three-hole punch
- ☐ Staples
- ☐ Staple puller

Equipment

- ☐ Overhead projector
- ☐ Projection screen
- ☐ Easel(s)
- ☐ Video player and monitor (check those needed)
    - ○ 8mm
    - ○ Super 8
    - ○ VHS
    - ○ SVHS
    - ○ Beta
    - ○ U-matic
- ☐ Connecting cables
- ☐ Video equipment cart
- ☐ 16mm film projector
- ☐ Projector cart
- ☐ Extension cords
- ☐ Adaptor plugs
- ☐ Spare projector lamps
- ☐ Pointer
- ☐ Chalkboard
- ☐ Whiteboard
- ☐ Podium
- ☐ Lectern
- ☐ Microphone(s)
- ☐ Name of technician _____ Phone _____

Other

- ☐ _____
- ☐ _____
- ☐ _____
- ☐ _____

Workshop Agenda Template

Agenda	Topics Key Points	Time Allotted	Start	Stop	Training Method	Media	Sourcebook Pages
1 Start-up	Welcome Housekeeping						
2 Agenda	Schedule Key topics Objectives						
3 Introductions							
4 Ice breaker							
5 Core Material							
6 Lunch							
7 Energizer							
8 Core Material							
9 Break							
10 Core material							
11 Evaluations							
12 Adjourn							

Participant Roster Worksheet

Workshop Title _____

Trainer(s) _____

Date _____**Time** _____

Location _____

_____

	Participant Name	**Extension**	**Department**
1	_____	_____	_____
2	_____	_____	_____
3	_____	_____	_____
4	_____	_____	_____
5	_____	_____	_____
6	_____	_____	_____
7	_____	_____	_____
8	_____	_____	_____
9	_____	_____	_____
10	_____	_____	_____
11	_____	_____	_____
12	_____	_____	_____
13	_____	_____	_____
14	_____	_____	_____
15	_____	_____	_____
16	_____	_____	_____
17	_____	_____	_____
18	_____	_____	_____
19	_____	_____	_____
20	_____	_____	_____
21	_____	_____	_____
22	_____	_____	_____

Room Setup

Room setup depends on the group's size and room's physical characteristics. Configurations include:

U-shape. The U-shape is recommended for groups of 10 to 20 people. Avoid seating people inside the U.

Angled rows. Suitable for groups of 20 or more. Arrange rectangular tables seating two or three people in a chevron pattern.

Leave aisles that are wide enough that you can comfortably move around the room.

Round tables. Round tables that seat four to five people are suitable for when group size is 12 or more. Arrange chairs so that each participant faces the facilitator.

Audiovisual equipment

The facilitator's table, easels, and videocassette player (if needed) should be positioned for clear viewing by all participants. If you have one, adjust the sound system so that everyone can hear videos, films, words spoken into a microphone, or whatever functions you are going to use.

Power source

Locate the climate control, light switches, electrical outlets, and sound system controls. Also, obtain the name of the technician to call for assistance.

Supplies, refreshments

Place one table to the side for materials, supplies, and items such as a three-hole punch, stapler, and staple puller. If refreshments will be served, set those up on a second side table.

Facilities

Locate the phones, rest rooms, vending machines, and cafeteria so that you can direct participants to them. Get names of nearby lunch spots if lunch is not provided.

Facilitator Preparation

Follow these steps to prepare to facilitate the workshop:

1   Review this sourcebook to become familiar with the background material, training designs, handouts, overhead transparency masters, leading activities, and assessments/instruments.

2   Review workshop plans with your client.

3   Select and duplicate handout masters from Chapter 7.

4   Select and duplicate transparency masters from Chapter 10.

5   Create hand-lettered charts.

6   Preview any films or videos, and read the accompanying leader's guides.

7   Practice and time your remarks, using a videotape recorder, audio tape, or mirror as a feedback device. Better yet, rehearse your presentation before a few colleagues who can provide constructive suggestions.

8   Learn to operate the audiovisual equipment and make sure it works.

On Day of the Workshop

Here is how to handle arrival of that fatal day.

☑ **Arrive 30 to 40 minutes early.**

Give yourself enough time to take care of all necessary details—including the unexpected. Make sure to allow a few moments for yourself before the participants arrive.

☑ **Test audiovisual equipment.**

Make sure that you are familiar with the audiovisual equipment, and that it is in working order, positioned properly, and in focus.

☑ **Check to see that the video or film is cued properly.**

Videos and film, if used, should be positioned at the starting point, ready to play.

Conducting the Workshop

The following pages describe general techniques useful in facilitating workshops.

Build Rapport

To build rapport with the participants:

☑ **Extend a warm welcome.**

Welcome participants with a warm smile and a handshake.

☑ **Call people by name.**

Learn and use participants' first names.

☑ **Show interest.**

Express interest in each individual. Find out what your students want to learn.

☑ **Relax and have fun.**

Show your sense of humor.

☑ **Be approachable.**

Be accepting of participant comments and available to participants at breaks and lunch.

☑ **Look and listen.**

Watch for participants' nonverbal messages such as puzzled looks or signs of discomfort. Listen to their comments and acknowledge their contributions.

Establish Credibility

☑ **Look professional.**

Wear clean, pressed clothing that reflects the dress standards of the organization, the group you are training, the training site, and your gender. Pay attention to your hair, nails, and makeup. Good grooming creates a neat appearance that helps establish professional credibility.

☑ **Know your subject.**

Study the background information in Chapter 2, the workshop scripts, and the directions for facilitating the learning activities and the assessments and instruments.

☑ **Speak clearly, distinctly, smoothly, and with authority.**

Avoid slang, jargon, profanity, or other language that might offend. Verbal qualifiers such as "kind of" or "sort of" detract from your credibility. "Ums" and "ahs" convey the impression that you are unsure of your material.

☑ **Maintain good posture.**

Communicate self-confidence and high self-esteem nonverbally by maintaining good posture.

☑ **Maintain eye contact.**

Look participants in the eye when you address them, as well as when you listen to their comments.

☑ **Use gestures for emphasis.**

Gestures can underscore key points, and make stories come alive.

Showing Overhead Transparencies

Glance at the screen to verify that the overhead transparency is positioned on the projector properly. Place a pen or pointer on the transparency next to the words or images that you want to emphasize. Alternatively, direct the viewers' attention to the screen behind you with the aid of a pointer, while continuing to face your audience. If you talk to the screen, participants won't be able to hear your comments.

Leading Discussions

Discussion questions and suggested answers can be found in the scripts for the one-day, half-day, and one-hour workshops, as well as in the directions that accompany the learning activities and the instruments and assessments. Some techniques for leading discussions follow.

☑ **Encourage idea exchange.**

Encourage participants to share ideas, experiences, supervision techniques, and systems knowledge, as well as to exchange opinions.

☑ **Involve everyone.**

Draw out shy or quiet individuals by giving them assignments; for instance, ask them to serve as recorder of the small group discussions.

☑ **Stay focused on the topic.**

Keep discussion focused on the topic. If a comment is off the subject, redirect it. You can also offer to discuss the matter during a break. If the point is on the topic that you will cover later, defer it.

☑ **Keep discussion positive.**

Keep discussions positive and constructive. If participants complain about their bosses or about the enterprise's policies, let them ventilate briefly. Then acknowledge their feelings and direct attention back to workshop objectives, saying something like, "It sounds like you find your situation frustrating. However, we can't change… (the organization's policy, your boss's management style, etc.), so, let's focus on those things within our control and our workshop topics. Look for ways to apply what you are learning today to your work unit."

Questions and Answers

The scripted workshops and many of the learning activities include questions you can ask, along with possible answers. Some techniques for facilitating question-and-answer sessions follow.

- Ask for volunteers to respond to questions.

- When someone gives an incorrect response, be tactful, to avoid causing embarrassment. Often, you can thank the respondent and continue accepting answers from others. When the preferred answers are given, support those answers. If letting an incorrect answer stand will misguide the students, then set the record straight diplomatically.

When participants ask you questions:

- Answer, but don't get carried off the subject.

- Instead of answering, pose the question to the group, ask what other participants think, encouraging participants to answer for each other.

- If you are unable to provide an answer, say so. Offer alternatives such as asking if others know the answer, suggesting where the participant might find an answer, or promising to obtain the information.

Maintain the Schedule

To cover all the workshop material within the allotted time, it is essential to stay on schedule. During group exercises, circulate and participate briefly in each group's discussions. This keeps the participants alert and ensures that they are completing the assignment. If a group is proceeding slowly relative to the other teams, urge it to pick up the pace.

Workshop Follow-Up

The following post-workshop activities help reinforce the training for each participant—and begin the preparation process for subsequent workshops:

☑ **Tabulate participant evaluations and provide your client with the results.**

A sample evaluation for the participants to complete at the conclusion of the workshop can be found in Chapter 9, "Instruments and Assessments." This is "Leadership Self-Assessment (Other)" on page 167.

☑ **Keep material current.**

Make any necessary changes before delivering the workshop again.

☑ **Mail participants' action plans.**

If you collected copies of participants' action plans, mail them as reminders of their self-binding contracts.

☑ **Plan reinforcement session.**

To be most effective, a reinforcement session should be planned as an integral part of the workshop.

Certificate of Achievement

This certifies that

_____
(name)

successfully completed the

Leadership Workshop

on

_____
(date)

Congratulations!

_____
(facilitator)

_____
(training manager)

Leadership Workshop

participant name

Leadership Workshop

participant name

Chapter Four

One-Day Leadership Workshop

This *Leadership: ASTD Sourcebook* chapter provides a training plan you can use to structure a one-day leadership workshop. Use it *as is*, or tailor it to your needs. Many users will want to run it once or twice as written. Then, based on feedback from the sessions and your own experience as a facilitator or observer, modify it to your situation.

This Chapter

... has these parts:

Workshop "Purpose and Objectives" below

"Workshop Agendas" on page 60

Workshop "Materials Needed" starts on page 62

"Suggested Flipcharts" on page 63

Step-by-step "Training Plan" on page 65.

Purpose and Objectives

This workshop introduces participants to the topic of leadership. On completion of the workshop, they will be able to:

- Describe the *characteristics* of a leader.
- Differentiate between *leadership* and *management*.
- Develop a *vision.*
- Describe the characteristics of a compelling *vision statement.*
- Identify tactics required to *keep a vision in the minds* of followers.
- Use staffing and coaching tactics that enable followers to work to *achieve* the vision.
- List ways that leaders lead by *example.*
- Be able to encourage individuals and the entire team by providing appropriate feedback.

Workshop Agendas

1 Workshop Introduction	Minutes 60	Start/Stop 8:00 / 9:00	Actual Start / Stop	
"Welcome and Introductions " on page 65	10	8:00 / 8:10	————	————
"Workshop Structure " on page 66	5	8:10 / 8:15	————	————
"Agenda and Logistics " on page 66	5	8:15 / 8:20	————	————
"Roles and Responsibilities " on page 66	10	8:20 / 8:30	————	————
"Assessment" on page 67, fill out, score	30	8:30 / 9:00	————	————

2 What Is Leadership?	Minutes 70	Start/Stop 9:00 / 10:10	Actual Start / Stop	
"Leaders We've Known " on page 68	15	9:00 / 9:15	————	————
"Leadership Characteristics " on page 68	10	9:15 / 9:25	————	————
"Types of Leaders " on page 69	10	9:25 / 9:35	————	————
"Leadership and Management " on page 69	20	9:35 / 9:55	————	————
Break	15	9:55 / 10:10	————	————

3 It Starts with a Vision	Minutes 65	Start/Stop 10:10 / 11:15	Actual Start / Stop	
"What Is Vision?" on page 71	5	10:10 / 10:15	————	————
"Life Path" on page 72	15	10:15 / 10:30	————	————
"Characteristics of Vision " on page 72	5	10:30 / 10:35	————	————
"Figures of Speech " on page 72	10	10:35 / 10:45	————	————
"Slogans" on page 74	10	10:45 / 10:55	————	————
"Communicating the Vision " on page 74	20	10:55 / 11:15	————	————

4 People Make It Happen	**Minutes 150**	**Start/Stop 11:15 / 1:45**	**Actual Start / Stop**	
"Roles and Responsibilities " on page 75	10	11:15 / 11:25	————	————
"People's Preferences " on page 76	30	11:25 / 11:55	————	————
Lunch	60	11:55 / 12:55		
"The Role of Training " on page 77	20	12:55 / 1:15	————	————
"The Role of Coaching " on page 78	30	1:15 / 1:45	————	————

5 Demonstrating Commitment	**Minutes 60**	**Start/Stop 1:45 / 2:45**	**Actual Start / Stop**	
"The Role of Example " on page 79	15	1:45 / 2:00	————	————
"The Signals We Send " on page 80	10	2:00 /2:10	————	————
"Involvement vs. Overcontrol " on page 80	20	2:10 / 2:30	————	————
Break	15	2:30 / 2:45	————	————

6 Motivating the Team	**Minutes 90**	**Start/Stop 2:45 / 4:15**	**Actual Start / Stop**	
"Recognition" on page 82	15	2:45 / 3:00	————	————
"What to Notice" on page 83	10	3:00 / 3:10	————	————
"Providing Positive Feedback " (individual) on page 83	20	3:10 / 3:30	————	————
"Providing Constructive Feedback " (individual on page 84)	30	3:30 / 4:00	————	————
"Celebrating Milestones " on page 85	15	4:00 / 4:15	————	————

7 Personal Commitment	**Minutes 30**	**Start/Stop 4:15 / 4:45**	**Actual Start / Stop**	
"Personal Goals" on page 86	15	4:15 / 4:30	————	————
"Recognition Activity" on page 86	15	4:30 / 4:45	————	————

Materials Needed

Following are checklists of materials recommended for the one-day leadership workshop. Masters for these materials are found in Chapters 7, 8, and 9 of this book. Unless otherwise noted:

Make one handout and instrument per participant.

Make one overhead transparency of each one needed.

Prepare one of each flipchart needed.

Handouts

Complete items on this checklist.

❑ "Leadership Characteristics" on page 110

❑ "A Leader I've Known" on page 112

❑ "Recognizing Leadership" on page 113

❑ "Types of Leaders" on page 115

❑ "Management and Leadership" on page 116

❑ "How Vision Develops" on page 121

❑ "How to Communicate the Vision" on page 123

❑ "Roles and Responsibilities" on page 125

❑ "Tailor Your Coaching" on page 126

❑ "Training the Team" on page 128

❑ "Autonomy and Control" on page 129

❑ "Motivating the Team" on page 130

❑ "Giving Positive Feedback" on page 132

❑ "Giving Constructive Feedback" on page 133

Activities

❑ "Life Path" on page 139

❑ "Images Are Everywhere" on page 141

❑ "Finding Out People's Preferences" on page 153

❑ "You're Signaling" on page 159

❑ "Giving Constructive Feedback" on page 161

Instruments and assessments

❑ "Coaching Assessment Questionnaire" on page 177

❑ "Goal Setting Self-Assessment Guidelines" on page 179

❑ "Leadership Characteristics" on page 180

Overheads

- ❏ "One-Day Leadership Workshop" on page 190
- ❏ "Leadership Characteristics" on page 193
- ❏ "Giving Positive Feedback" on page 194
- ❏ "Agenda and Logistics" on page 195
- ❏ "Vision Defined" on page 196
- ❏ "Communicating the Vision" on page 197
- ❏ "Build on Strengths" on page 198
- ❏ "Autonomy and Control" on page 199
- ❏ "Motivate the Team" on page 200

Suggested Flipcharts

Welcome

to

Building the Vision

One-Day Leadership Training

Preferred Emphasis

Note participant expectations on this flipchart.

Use different colored pens for each line/input.

If feasible, put requester's initials beside each request.

You will post this flipchart and return to it at the end of the session.

At the end of the session, ask participants to evaluate how the session met their needs.

Slogans

If the organization has a slogan, list it first.

List well-known slogans, many of which have been used by politicians.

Leadership Example:

Behaviors

List whatever the participants come up with, which may include:

> Punctuality
>
> First to arrive, last to leave
>
> Traveling coach fare, etc.

Milestones

List milestones the group identifies, which may include:

> End of planning stage
>
> Prototype review
>
> End of alpha or beta testing
>
> Approval into production
>
> Internal launch of the product or process

Celebration Ideas

Participants will identify many, which may include:

> Party
>
> Outing
>
> Bowling
>
> Roast
>
> Goodies for break
>
> Lottery tickets
>
> Movie tickets
>
> Dinner out, etc.

Training Plan

1 . . . *Introduction to the Workshop (8:00 to 9:00)*

Purpose

This workshop section establishes an environment in which participants and workshop facilitator are at ease with each other, and in which all have a clear understanding of what is expected of them, and what to expect of the workshop.

Objectives

On completion of this workshop segment, participants will be able to:

- View the workshop setting as one of active involvement.
- Describe the flow and duration of the workshop.
- Understand the expectations for participation in the session.
- Identify the other participants in the session.
- Name leadership characteristics.
- Cite leadership characteristics which they typically practice.
- Explain their own objectives for the training session.

AGENDA: Workshop Introduction	Minutes 60	Start/Stop 8:00 / 9:00	Actual Start / Stop	
"Welcome and Introductions " on page 65	10	8:00 / 8:10	_____	_____
"Workshop Structure " on page 66	5	8:10 / 8:15	_____	_____
"Agenda and Logistics " on page 66	5	8:15 / 8:20	_____	_____
"Roles and Responsibilities " on page 66	10	8:20 / 8:30	_____	_____
"Assessment" on page 67, fill out, score	30	8:30 / 9:00	_____	_____

00:10   **Welcome and Introductions**

HAVE the "Welcome" flipchart on page 63 posted prominently at the front of the room.

WELCOME the participants to the session and make these points:

This is a full one-day workshop which will be interesting and profitable to you.

Thank you for taking the time from your busy schedule.

INTRODUCE yourself briefly, tell participants about your background, and explain your interest in leadership by relating an anecdote about a leader you have known who made an impression on you.

ASK participants to write their names in bold letters on the tent cards, fold and place them at their places.

HAVE participants briefly introduce themselves, by telling their names and *where* in the organization they work.

00:05

Workshop Structure

REVIEW the workshop, while showing the overhead transparency "One-Day Leadership Workshop" on page 190. Make these points:

- Starting with how you currently practice leadership, we review the characteristics that we generally ascribe to leaders.

- In the process of doing this, we will draw on your experiences, review case studies, and practice some of the skills.

- You are an integral part of what will make this workshop successful. Your active participation is a fundamental requirement to the workshop's success.

00:05

Agenda and Logistics

REVIEW the "Agenda and Logistics" on page 195 overhead.

DISCUSS the following:

- Topics to be covered in the morning and the afternoon.
- Location of restrooms, telephones, smoking areas, etc.
- Arrangements for refreshments, lunch, handling messages, etc.
- The necessity for promptness, full participation.

ACKNOWLEDGE that the amount of material to be covered may cause you to cut some discussion. Explain that you will do this in the interest of time and of keeping the pace interesting for all.

00:10

Roles and Responsibilities

MAKE these points:

As facilitator, my role is to guide discussions, facilitate the full involvement of all, and keep the pace of the workshop interesting and stimulating.

Your role is to:

- Examine and analyze ideas.
- Test theories and concepts.

- Practice new skills in a safe environment.

You may *find that you don't* understand someone or something, that you *disagree* with a point, or that you *want further information*. Feel comfortable asking for what you need.

All of us will practice respect for one another by listening attentively to others, not talking when others are, speaking clearly so that all can hear, and returning promptly from breaks.

00:30   ## Assessment

 REFER to the assessment "Leadership Self-Assessment (Other)" on page 167.

SAY something like the following as a way of introducing the assessment:

- Take a moment to describe how you interact with people, situations, and ideas.

- Answer each question by indicating how often the statement is true for you.

ALLOW participants five to ten minutes to complete the questionnaire. When most are finished, tell them how to score it, using the "Rating Your Self-Assessment Scores" on page 169.

 REFER to the handout "Leadership Characteristics" on page 110.

ASK participants to read the complete descriptor of each leadership characteristic and make notes beneath the profile, graphing their scores for each characteristic.

 ASK volunteers to explain what they want to gain from this session, based on their understanding of leadership characteristics, and their own profile.

NOTE participant requests on a flipchart entitled "Preferred Emphasis" on page 63. Include initials of requesters after each.

POST the flipchart prominently on a wall. Throughout the day, tie topics and activities to it.

 ASK if there are any questions. When appropriate, transition to the next section.

2.... *What Is Leadership? (9:00 to 10:10)*

Purpose

The purpose of this part of the workshop is to identify what is unique about leaders, when viewed in terms of people we know.

Objectives

It will enable participants to be able to:

- Identify leaders they have known, and how they exemplified the characteristics of leaders.
- Identify the characteristics that differentiate leaders from those who just manage.
- Describe how, in other cultures, leadership qualities may differ.

AGENDA: What Is Leadership?	Minutes 70	Start/Stop 9:00 / 10:10	Actual Start / Stop	
"Leaders We've Known" on page 68	15	9:00 / 9:15	_____	_____
"Leadership Characteristics" on page 68	10	9:15 / 9:25	_____	_____
"Types of Leaders" on page 69	10	9:25 / 9:35	_____	_____
"Leadership and Management" on page 69	20	9:35 / 9:55	_____	_____
Break	15	9:55 / 10:10	_____	_____

00:15

Leaders We've Known

PASS out the handout "A Leader I've Known" on page 112.

ASK participants to take a moment to think about a leader they have known. Have them jot down what this person did that they think indicated his or her leadership. Allow 3-5 minutes.

LEAD a round robin in which each person describes a leader and his/her actions.

CHECK OFF leadership characteristics discussed. Use the overhead transparency "Leadership Characteristics" on page 193. Place a hash mark beside the characteristics that the behaviors being described denote.

00:10

Leadership Characteristics

REVIEW the handout "Recognizing Leadership" on page 113.

When participants have finished the handout and the questions that follow it, briefly discuss it using points such as:

WHAT character traits would you say most leaders share? I'm defining character traits such as timidity and gentleness.

You're looking for:

> *Courage, self-assurance, openness to diversity,*
> *willingness to be wrong, determination, generosity, persistence,*
> *convictions, caring.*

 ARE good management skills a requirement for leaders?

You're looking for:

> *They're not a requirement, but they sure help a leader be effective*
> *in achieving his/her vision.*

 HOW do we nurture our own ability to be leaders?

You're looking for:

> *Pay attention to our own opinions, act on our ideas, discuss our*
> *ideas with others and listen to their input, try things out, give up*
> *being afraid of being wrong.*

Types of Leaders

00:10

 INTRODUCE this topic by asking questions such as:

- If leaders all have such wonderful character traits, it should follow that all of them are admirable characters, right?

  Allow some discussion. You're looking for the recognition that the leaders' values influence their actions.

- Do leaders only appear in highly democratic or autonomous environments?

  You're looking for an awareness that leaders emerge in all cultures, just as no personality type has a corner on leadership. Leadership characteristics can be practiced by people of all personality styles and all types of values.

 HAVE participants read the handout "Types of Leaders" on page 115.

Leadership and Management

00:20

MAKE these points:

- We've said that leaders usually possess some management skills, but that managers do not necessarily possess leadership characteristics.

- Now is the time to identify the defining differences between the two.

- Note that this in no way implies that one is better or more important than the other.

- It is true however, that in the past management often has been *emphasized* and leadership *ignored*.

 ORGANIZE participants for a table group activity. Introduce it by saying something like:

> We've talked a lot about the *characteristics* of leaders, how they *differ*, and what they *share* in common.

REFLECT now on how *leaders* differ from *managers*.

> In this activity, your table groups will consider a list of characteristics. As groups, agree on which characteristics define *management* and which describe *leadership*:

 TELL participants to follow these guidelines:

- Read the list of skills and characteristics on the handout "Management and Leadership" on page 116.

- Individually decide in which category each one resides.

- As a group, compare notes, then discuss and come to a consensus about the characteristics on which you differ.

 CALL TIME after about 8-10 minutes.

 TELL table groups to share their conclusions with the group at large.

 REVIEW the table group discussion by asking questions such as:

- Why bother making such distinctions?

- Where did you disagree?

 DISCUSS the items on which there is disagreement, asking participants to support their own choices.

CONCLUDE by reiterating that effective leaders need good management skills, and good managers should endeavor to develop leadership abilities.

15:00   ***BREAK***

3 . . . *It Starts with a Vision (10:10 to 11:15)*

Purpose   Focus on what is meant by *vision* and why it's important.

Objectives   On completion, participants will be able to:

- Identify what vision *is* and why it's *important*.
- Recognize that we all have the ability to *visualize*.
- Use *vivid images* to reinforce the vision.
- Recognize important aspects of *communicating* a vision.
- List ways a vision can be *reinforced* in various work setting.

AGENDA: It Starts with a Vision	Minutes 65	Start/Stop 10:10 / 11:15	Actual Start / Stop	
"What Is Vision?" on page 71	5	10:10 / 10:15	_____	_____
"Life Path" on page 72	15	10:15 / 10:30	_____	_____
"Characteristics of Vision " on page 72	5	10:30 / 10:35	_____	_____
"Figures of Speech " on page 72	10	10:35 / 10:45	_____	_____
"Slogans" on page 74	10	10:45 / 10:55	_____	_____
"Communicating the Vision " on page 74	20	10:55 / 11:15	_____	_____

00:05   ## What Is Vision?

ASK participants to close their eyes and think about a vivid childhood memory. When all have had a moment to recall, lead a discussion by asking questions such as:

- What is that memory like? Can you see it? Is there color? Is it an emotion? How would you describe the memory

  You're looking for descriptions such as a mental snapshot, feeling, detailed, instant awareness.

- Did you see a picture?

  Most will say yes.

- You can have a vivid mental picture when you look backwards, Do you do the same thing looking forward?

  There may be a variety of responses.

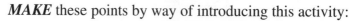

00:15

Life Path

MAKE these points by way of introducing this activity:

- Writers and psychologists contend that we do a better job of looking into the future when we take stock of our past.

- In this activity, I want you to illustrate your life path.

REFER participants to the activity "Life Path" on page 139, and have them illustrate it using the guidelines for that activity.

TELL participants to follow these guidelines:

- Place an "X" to denote where you are on this highway.

- Place five illustrations—icons, symbols, road signs, bill boards—representing major influences up to this point in your life. Influences can be events, relationships, responsibilities, etc.

- Place five more illustrations to denote upcoming attractions on the route of your journey. The attractions don't have to be major, nor need they necessarily be way into the future, merely something you dream about or wish for.

CALL TIME after about 8-10 minutes.

TELL participants to share their illustrations among their table groups. Allow about 5 minutes.

DEBRIEF the activity.

REVIEW the table group discussion by asking questions such as:

- Were you able to identify five images from your future?

- How far into the future did you go?

- Would you agree that you can visualize some things in your life? How would you describe the things that you can visualize?

  You're looking for responses such as—things that are personally important, we find attractive, make us feel good.

00:05

Characteristics of Vision

HAVE participants read the handout "How Vision Develops" on page 121.

SHOW the overhead "Vision Defined" on page 196 to review the reading.

00:10

Figures of Speech

INTRODUCE the topic by asking questions such as:

- Who can tell me what a *metaphor* is?

  Describes one thing as or in terms of another, e.g., "A mighty fortress is our God," "A torrent of abuse," etc.

- And—again going back to literature—can anyone define *simile*?

  A simile compares two unlike things, uses the word like, e.g., "She is like a rose."

- What about an *analogy*?

  The partial similarity between two dissimilar things is used to make a point, e.g., the heart and a pump, adult and children's behavior.

- When you were back in school, you probably associated *metaphors* and *similes* with poets and poetry. But the highway signs you just completed may have had several visual metaphors in them. In fact, figures of speech occur in *everyday life*.

 TELL participants to review the list of metaphors and similes on the activity sheet "Images Are Everywhere" on page 141.

 TELL participants to follow these guidelines:

- Individually, read the list of figures of speech.

- As a group, decide what is being described by each figure of speech.

- Decide through discussion on a positive, work related outcome or pattern of behavior you wish to describe.

- Develop a figure of speech to describe it.

 CALL TIME after about 12 minutes.

DEBRIEF the activity "Figures of Speech Activity Guidelines" on page 140.

 REVIEW the table group discussion by doing the following:

- Call out the number of each item on the list. Call on one table group to identify the feeling or behavior pattern described. Call on the other groups to *agree, disagree, modify, amplify.*

- When the review is complete call on each table group to share its figures of speech.

- After each is read aloud ask the rest of the group to identify what this figure of speech brings to mind. Then have the "owners" describe the action or behavior pattern they wanted to describe.

- When all groups have finished, ask participants to discuss the activity—how difficult was it, how effective the figures of speech were in creating mental images and conveying meaning.

  You're looking for: images are hard to think of without practice, are very effective (involve the listener).

00:10

Slogans

MAKE these points to introduce the topic:

- Leaders often use *short phrases* to reinforce their vision.
- These *slogans* are usually a *call to solidarity* and to *action*.
- We're exposed to them all the time, particularly from *politicians*.
- Can you identify slogans that you are familiar with from either everyday life or the workplace?

NOTE participant responses on a flipchart. (An example, "Slogans," is on page 64.) If necessary, jump start the conversation with slogans such as

- "One 'man' (politically incorrect!) one vote!"
- "A chicken in every pot."
- "All for one and one for all."
- "Ask not…" etc.

CONCLUDE the activity by asking participants to suggest why leaders use such slogans.

00:20

Communicating the Vision

SHOW the overhead "Vision Defined" on page 196.

MAKE these points:

- When leaders communicate their vision, they use many of the processes you have just used:
- They envision a future event in vivid detail.
- They capture the essence of that vision in colorful and evocative language, to which their audience can relate.
- They use a slogan or catch phrase throughout, as a refrain.
- That slogan is often used as a rallying cry to reinforce the vision and keep it refreshed in the minds of their followers.
- They reinforce the vision in numerous ways, constantly.

TAKE a moment to review the handout "How to Communicate the Vision" on page 123.

CONCLUDE by reiterating that vision is a leader's deeply felt commitment. It must be communicated vividly and reinforced at every turn. It is the bond which binds the leader and his/her followers.

4 . . . People Make It Happen (11:15 to 1:45)

Purpose   This workshop section reinforces the idea that vision is only realized through the efforts of followers who commit to it.

Objectives   When they complete this workshop segment, participants should know:

- Why defining and tailoring roles and responsibilities is important.
- How tapping into people's preferences adds to their commitment.
- The leader's responsibility to train followers in essential skills.
- Tailor coaching to the needs of various team members.

AGENDA: People Make It Happen	Minutes 150	Start/Stop 11:15 / 1:45	Actual Start / Stop	
"Roles and Responsibilities " on page 75	10	11:15 / 11: 25	————	————
"People's Preferences " on page 76	30	11:25 / 11:55	————	————
Lunch	60	11:55 / 12:55		
"The Role of Training " on page 77	20	12:55 / 1:15	————	————
"The Role of Coaching " on page 78	30	1:15 / 1:45	————	————

00:10

Roles and Responsibilities

INTRODUCE the topic by asking participants what team sports they enjoy. When people offer their responses (soccer, football, basketball, etc.) ask them to imagine for a moment that we are going to change the rules of that game—all players have equal responsibility, they should do what they are best at, what they are capable of doing, and work totally "democratically."

ASK:

- How do you think this would work?

   You're looking for responses such as: *"No, people need to have assigned responsibilities," "some people would do everything and others would be left out," "people would get in each other's way," etc.*

- Why do we need roles?

   It helps us accomplish more working together. People are more involved when they feel responsible for something. People with special skills are better at some tasks than others, etc.

● What's important when assigning a role and a responsibility to someone?

There may be a variety of responses. You're looking for: *"knowing what to do," "being able to execute the task," "getting the training needed,"* etc.

 ASK participants to read the handout, "Roles and Responsibilities" on page 125.

00:30

People's Preferences

 INTRODUCE the activity by making a case for focusing on the people—followers—who may carry out much of the vision, by making these points:

● A leader usually relies on others to carry out his/her vision.

● Followers often volunteer for the role they play—doing something that matches their abilities, or for which they have enthusiasm.

● In a work setting, because of traditional ways of structuring job responsibilities, managers might ignore the necessity of making that match. A leader with good management skills would not.

 ASK, can you imagine a:

● Football coach selecting a 5-foot 5-inch tailback? Why not?

● Would a play director ignore the uniqueness of each actor's abilities when assigning parts?

● Why would leaders not assign people to responsibilities that match their talents?

 LISTEN to responses, then **MAKE** these statements:

● Matching people's strengths to job requirements may necessitate restructuring job responsibilities

● The advantage of tapping into people's strengths when making assignments is that people have greater enthusiasm and interest in what they are doing—it is intrinsically rewarding to them. They are not carried along by idealism and discipline alone.

 SHOW the overhead "Build on Strengths" on page 198 to review the disscussion.

 REFER participants to the activity "Finding Out People's Preferences" on page 153.

 TELL participants they will work in pairs to conduct this role play.

ASK participants to count off in twos. A *one* and a *two* constitute a working pair.

● Individually, read the directions.

- *Ones* start the interview. As you listen, take notes. If something is unclear, ask for:

    Clarification: *What do you mean by that? Could you say more about that?*

    An example: *Could you give me an example? Give me a "for instance"!*

- *Twos* answer the questions truthfully.
- You have 10 minutes for each round.

CALL TIME after 10 and 20 minutes.

00:60

DEBRIEF the activity.

REVIEW the role play experience by asking questions such as:

- How did it feel to be asked about your strengths—what you enjoy, what you're good at, what you learn easily?
- Do you do this at work? Why or why not?
- What implication does this have for roles and responsibilities?

60:00   **LUNCH BREAK**

00:20   **The Role of Training**

LEAD a large group discussion on the role of training by commenting and asking questions such as:

- Think of your favorite sports team—anyone want to volunteer the team? (Accept the most popular one offered.)
- How does (name of the team) select players? (Choose the best— really talented people—they can buy.)
- Does anyone know how many coaches the team has? (Usually three levels, 10 or more.)
- What do these coaches do?

    You're looking for: *"develop plays," "teach plays," "observe players," "advise players on how to improve," "give players individual development plans," "require progress," "keep score," etc.*

- What happens before the season?

    You're looking for: *"training camp—a concentrated period of learning how to play together," "review the basics," "develop an appropriate level of conditioning."*

ASK the following questions

Aren't these really good players to start with? Why do they need so much training and coaching? How are we different? What kind of training should we be doing?

HAVE participants read the handout "Training the Team" on page 128.

00:30

The Role of Coaching

INTRODUCE the topic by making these points:

- Coaching is the natural follow-up to training.
- Coaching usually connotes one-on-one.
- What other characteristics would you attribute to coaching?

  You're looking for: *"based on observation of the person being coached, and on his/her task results," "suited to that person's needs, experience, and motivation level."*

- What types of things would a coach get involved in with a team member?

  Problem solving: *the player is not getting a certain result he/she is striving for—routine operation, motivation.*

TELL participants to review the handout "Tailor Your Coaching" on page 126.

DISCUSS the handout briefly, answering any questions participants may have.

CONDUCT the assessment interview "Coaching Assessment Guidelines" on page 176 using the guidelines on page 176.

5 ... *Demonstrating Commitment (1:45 to 2:45)*

Purpose   This workshop section reflects on the leader's responsibility to lead by example.

Objectives   On completion, participants will be able to:

- Describe how example can motivate or de-motivate.
- Become attuned to the messages we convey through behavior.
- Determine how the leader can remain involved while allowing team members autonomy, and empowering them to make decisions.

AGENDA: Demonstrating Commitment	Minutes 60	Start/Stop 1:45 / 2:45	Actual Start / Stop	
"The Role of Example" on page 79	15	1:45 / 2:00	_____	_____
"The Signals We Send" on page 80	10	2:00 /2:10	_____	_____
"Involvement vs. Overcontrol " on page 80	20	2:10 / 2:30	_____	_____
Break	15	2:30 / 2:45	_____	_____

00:15

The Role of Example

INTRODUCE the leadership characteristic walking the talk by asking participants to think about how the behavior of others affects them. To stimulate discussion, ask questions such as:

- Has someone's positive behavior ever helped you act in a certain way?

   If it is necessary to stimulate participants' thinking, you may use a personal example, or you may mention someone who was particularly faithful to a diet, an exercise regimen, doing homework, etc.

   - When a participant describes a behavior example, ask what the person thought about it and how it affected his/her own actions.

- Has someone's negative behavior ever presented you with a challenge?

   - Invite two or three examples.

   - Question respondents to identify what negative effect the example had, and to clarify why the behavior had such an effect.

ASK participants to identify positive behaviors that they think leaders ought to demonstrate (Refer to "Leaders set example" on page 28.) List responses on a flipchart such as "Leadership Example: Behaviors" on page 64.

00:10   ## The Signals We Send

ASK participants to pick the name of one of their fellow participants and to complete the activity "You're Signaling" on page 159, for that person.

WARN participants that they should not overanalyze each statement lead-in. Where they cannot truthfully make a comment, they should simply write "no impression."

TELL participants to write on the top of the activity sheet the name they drew from the container. Make sure no one drew his/her own name.

ASK participants to answer questions with the first thing that pops into their minds, to not filter it.

CALL TIME after 5 minutes.

COLLECT papers.

DISTRIBUTE the "You're Signaling" sheets to the people whose names are written on the top.

GIVE participants a moment to read them.

DEBRIEF by *ASKING* participants to comment on:

- Did you have to think about what to write?
- Were you aware that you were gathering and processing so much information about others?
- Were you surprised by what you read about yourself?
- Do any of you feel that you don't want to send some of the signals that another received from you?

  If so, what will you do differently in the future?

00:20   ## Involvement vs. Overcontrol

INTRODUCE the topic by asking questions such as:

- Are controls necessary in a business environment? Explain your answers.

  Allow differing ideas to be voiced. Verify your understanding of points as they are made and ask for responses.

- In some environments, are controls more critical than in others? Name some, and explain why.

  You may expect the following: *controls are very necessary in lots of places with zero or low tolerance for error—aviation, health care, food preparation, etc.*

- If controls are necessary, what is overcontrol?

  Allow differences of opinion. You expect people to come to the conclusion that actions which demonstrate lack of trust in a person's ability to think, follow through, etc. represent overcontrol. Like coaching, what one person might regard as overcontrol, another may see as lax disregard.

 TELL participants to read "Autonomy and Control" on page 129.

 SHOW the overhead "Autonomy and Control" on page 199, leaving it on the screen while you discuss the reading.

DISCUSS the handout briefly, answering participant questions.

00:15   **Break**

6.... *Motivating the Team (2:45 to 4:15)*

Purpose

This workshop section highlights opportunities available to leaders to provide reinforcement.

Objectives

On completion of this workshop segment, participants should be able to:

- Describe how "recognizing" behavior is a powerful motivator.
- Use recognition as a way of creating a climate of excellence.
- Give positive feedback to fellow workers.
- Give corrective feedback in a constructive manner.
- List alternative ways of reinforcing team successes.

AGENDA: Motivating the Team	Minutes 90	Start/Stop 2:45 / 4:15	Actual Start / Stop	
"Recognition" on page 82	15	2:45 / 3:00	————	————
"What to Notice" on page 83	10	3:00 / 3:10	————	————
"Providing Positive Feedback" (individual) on page 83	20	3:10 / 3:30	————	————
"Providing Constructive Feedback" (individual on page 84)	30	3:30 / 4:00	————	————
"Celebrating Milestones" on page 85	15	4:00 / 4:15	————	————

00:15   # **Recognition**

SHOW the overhead "Motivate the Team" on page 200 while introducing the topic.

INTRODUCE the leadership characteristic motivating others by asking participants why people generally like to work on the projects of leaders.

> Expect to hear that leaders *appeal to ideals, are more motivated, are more appreciative, don't take people for granted,* etc.

EXPLAIN that *motivating others* is a result of a number of behaviors, which include:

- *recognizing* individuals on the team,
- *crediting* positive behavior and results,
- *correcting* problems quickly and constructively, and
- *celebrating* team successes.

ASK participants to review the handout "Motivating the Team" on page 130.

CONDUCT participant brainstorm of all the ways a leader can "recognize" a contributor/team member:

- Remind participants of brainstorming rules—no criticism!
- List ideas on flipchart.
- When ideas are spun out, ask participants to identify how many of these ideas are feasible to implement in the workplace.

00:10   **What to Notice**

INTRODUCE the concept of focusing on the positive, by asking questions such as:

- What is most typically noticed and commented on in your workplace?

  Anticipated answer: *what is wrong, problems, crises...*

- Why is that the case?

  Anticipated answer: *Most managers think that is their domain, mistakes cause problems, require management response.*

- What would happen if managers/leaders focused on the positive?

  Anticipated answer: *that behavior might recur more often.*

ASK participants to review the handout "Encouraging the Individual Team Member" on page 131.

QUESTION participants to verify that they have gotten the main points of intrinsic and extrinsic motivators from the reading.

TELL participants that a policy of focusing on the positive, paying attention to those who do the best work and get the best results, tends to cause:

- More of those wanted behaviors.
- A more positive work atmosphere.
- More energy and enthusiasm.
- Improved attendance.
- Higher performance.

00:20   **Providing Positive Feedback**

INTRODUCE the practice by giving these directions:

- Providing specific, positive feedback is the cheapest and most meaningful recognition you can give anyone.

ASK participants to read "Giving Positive Feedback" on page 132.

REVIEW the handout to assure that participants have understood why and how to provide positive feedback by asking questions such as:

- Why are leaders generous with the use of *crediting* or positive feedback?

- How does one give credit/positive feedback?

  You are looking for someone who will enumerate the steps.

 MODEL the practice by picking out one of the participants in the session. Demonstrate the skill by saying something like:

- **Step One:** (name of the person), *I want to compliment you on the way you* (have applied yourself in this training, paid attention when others are speaking, etc.).

- **Step Two:** *When Mary was speaking, you maintained eye contact, and you asked clarifying questions of Jim and Susan.*

- **Step Three:** *Listening in this way not only assures you of gaining a better understanding of others, but it also encourages those who are speaking.*

- **Step Four:** *Listening in this way is a powerful skill and one that is quite rare.*

 ASK for volunteers to demonstrate the skill.

ACCEPT one or two volunteers.

 POINT TO the skill steps on the overhead "Giving Positive Feedback" on page 194 as each person models the steps.

 ASK participants to whom you gave the feedback how the experience felt.

00:30

Providing Constructive Feedback

 **INTRODUCE** the topic by asking participants what constructive feedback might have to do with motivating team members.

You are looking for:

- *Standards are important to creating a motivated environment*

- *Team members become disheartened if one team member is not living up to the group's norms*

- *Challenge helps maintain interest*

TELL participants to read "Giving Constructive Feedback" on page 133.

DISCUSS the handout briefly, answering participant questions.

 CONDUCT the roleplay "Giving Constructive Feedback" on page 161 using the following procedures:

TELL participants they will work in pairs to conduct this practice activity.

ASK participants to count off in twos. A *one* and a *two* constitute a working pair. (Make sure people work with a different partner than in the last activity.)

- Individually, read the directions and prepare your statements and questions.
- *Twos* start the interview by giving *one's* background on the situation.
- *Ones* may improvise in responding to questions.
- Complete the feedback with an agreement.

CALL TIME for feedback at 7 minutes and round two at 10.

REVIEW the activity by asking questions such as:

- How did it feel to receive feedback?
- How did it feel to give feedback?
- Is it appropriate to give this type of feedback to peers?

ENCOURAGE some discussion.

00:15

Celebrating Milestones

INTRODUCE the brainstorm by asking participants to identify how it feels to successfully complete a project phase.

> *Accept a few responses.*

ASK participants to identify what phases or milestones they accomplish as part of their function.

LIST responses on the "Milestones" flipchart on page 64. Post it to one side.

CONDUCT a brainstorm of what leaders can do to celebrate accomplishing these interim steps. Record responses on "Celebration Ideas" flipchart seen on page 64.

7 . . . . Personal Commitment (4:15 to 4:45)

Purpose
This workshop section provides participants the opportunity to plan how they will apply what they have learned in the session.

Objectives
On completion of this workshop segment, participants will be able to:

- Tell how they expect to apply leadership practices discussed in this workshop.

- Apply the skills, and be motivated to do so.

AGENDA: Personal Commitment	Minutes 30	Start/Stop 4:15 / 4:45	Actual Start / Stop	
"Personal Goals" on page 86	15	4:15 / 4:30	————	————
"Recognition Activity" on page 86	15	4:30 / 4:45	————	————

00:15

Personal Goals

ASK participants to read "Goal Setting Self-Assessment Guidelines" on page 179, and to fill out the assessment and worksheet.

> While participants are doing this, list one point for each participant on which you can credit them.

00:15

Recognition Activity

CALL each participant to come forward to receive his or her "Certificate of Achievement" on page 56.

GIVE the participant positive feedback on some aspect of his or participation.

ASK others who wish to credit this person to do so while he or she is still at the front of the room.

THANK the group for its participation.

Chapter Five:

Half-Day Leadership Workshop

This *Leadership: ASTD Trainer's Sourcebook* chapter provides a training plan you can use to structure a half-day leadership workshop. Use it *as is*, or tailor it to your needs. A good plan of action is to run it once or twice *as written*. Then, based on feedback from the sessions and your own experience as a trainer or an observer of the trainer, modify it to your own situation.

This Chapter

... has these parts:

Workshop "Purpose and Objectives" below

"Workshop Agenda" on page 88

Workshop "Materials Needed" on page 89

"Suggested Flipcharts" on page 90

Step-by-step half-day "Training Plan" on page 91.

Purpose and Objectives

This workshop provides an in-depth leadership visioning experience—it's sources, how to enable and communicate it. On completion, participants will be able to:

- *Describe* the characteristic of challenging the status quo.

- *Recognize* one's own preferences and values.

- *Visualize* a future event.

- *Describe* the characteristics of a compelling vision statement.

- *Acknowledge* the need for risk taking when implementing a vision.

- *Identify* tactics required to keep a vision active in followers' minds.

Workshop Agenda

1 **Introduction to the Workshop**	Minutes 60	Start/Stop 8:00/9:00	Actual Start / Stop	
"Welcome and Introductions " on page 91	10	8:00 / 8:10		
"Overview of the Workshop " on page 92	5	8:10 / 8:15		
"Agenda and Logistics " on page 92	5	8:15 / 8:20		
"Roles and Responsibilities " on page 93	10	8:20 / 8:30		
"Assessment" on page 93; fill out, score	30	8:30 / 9:00		

2 **Questioning Groupthink**	Minutes 75	Start/Stop 9:00/10:15	Actual Start / Stop	
"Know What We Think " on page 95	10	9:00 / 9:10		
"Know What We Value " on page 95	30	9:10 / 9:40		
"Act on Our Insights " on page 96	10	9:40 / 9:50		
"Listening" on page 97	10	9:50 / 10:00		
Break	15	10:00 / 10:15		

3 **Develop a Vision**	Minutes 100	Start/Stop 10:15/11:55	Actual Start / Stop	
"Time Travel—a Visualization " on page 98	20	10:15 / 10:35		
"Risk Taking" on page 100	20	10:35 / 10:55		
"Communicating Your Vision " on page 101	10	10:55 / 11:05		
"Keeping Your Vision Alive " on page 101	30	11:05 / 11:35		
"Commitments" on page 101	10	11:35 / 11:45		
"Recognition Activity " on page 102	10	11:45 / 11:55		

Materials Needed

Following are checklists of materials recommended for the half-day leadership workshop. Masters for these materials are found in Chapters 7 through 10 of this book. Unless otherwise noted:

Make one copy of each handout, activity, or instrument per participant.

Make one overhead transparency of each one needed.

Prepare flipchart titles needed.

Handouts

❑ "Openness and Vision" on page 117

❑ "Leaders Learn by Listening" on page 119

❑ "How to Communicate the Vision" on page 123

❑ "Commitment and Follow-Up" on page 135

❑ "Which One is a Vision" on pages 149-151. You can use this as an alternate to "I Think I Can" on page 157.

Instruments and assessments

Use where indicated:

❑ "Listening Assessment (Self)" on page 173

❑ "Information Gathering (Self)" on page 183

Activities

❑ "A Few of My Favorite Things" on page 143

❑ "It's Up to Us to Decide" on page 146

❑ "Visualization Activity Guidelines"* on page 154

❑ "I Think I Can" on page 157

Overheads

❑ "A Half-Day Leadership Workshop" on page 191

❑ "Agenda and Logistics" on page 195

NOTE TO FACILITATOR: If your audience is more verbal and less symbolic, you could use "Which One is a Vision" on pages 150-151 instead of the activity above. Guidelines for the alternate activity are on page 149.

Suggested Flipcharts

Welcome

to

Building the Vision

Half-Day Leadership Training

It's Up to **You**

- Openness to material and one another
- Contribute—safe environment
- Let go—of old or safe habits
- Take risks, etc.

Preferred **Emphasis**

Note participant expectations on this flipchart.

- Use different colored pens for each line/input.
- If feasible, put requester's initials beside each request.
- You will post this flipchart and return to it at the end of the session.
- At the end of the session, ask participants to evaluate how the session met their needs.

Keeping **Vision** Alive

Note participant responses to discussion on this flipchart.

- Use different colored markers to distinguish suggestions from each other.
- Number the list
- When complete, comment on how many ways they know of to keep a vision alive.

Training Plan

Purpose   This workshop section establishes an environment in which participants and facilitator are at ease with each other, and in which participants have a clear understanding of what to expect and what is required of them.

Objectives   On completion of this workshop segment, participants should be able to:

- View the workshop setting as one of active involvement.

- Describe the flow and duration of the workshop.

- Understand the expectations for participation in the session.

- Identify the other participants in the session.

- Know the importance of vision.

- Define their personal objectives for the training session.

AGENDA: Introduction to the Workshop	Minutes 60	Start/Stop 8:00/9:00	Actual Start / Stop	
"Welcome and Introductions " on page 91	10	8:00 / 8:10	_____	_____
"Overview of the Workshop " on page 92	5	8:10 / 8:15	_____	_____
"Agenda and Logistics " on page 92	5	8:15 / 8:20	_____	_____
"Roles and Responsibilities " on page 93	10	8:20 / 8:30	_____	_____
"Assessment" on page 93: fill out, score	30	8:30 / 9:00	_____	_____

1 ... Introduction to the Workshop (8:00 to 9:00)

00:10

Welcome and Introductions

BEFORE participants arrive at the session, prepare a flipchart welcoming them and identifying the topic and length of this session. You also may develop a second flipchart that identifies the characteristics of the session environment.

WELCOME participants to the session and make these points:

- This is a full half-day workshop which focuses on the most distinguishing characteristic of leaders—*their vision.*

- Thank you for taking time from your busy schedules.

INTRODUCE yourself briefly, tell participants a little about your background, identifying your interest in the topic of leadership vision by relaying an anecdote about how you or someone you know has been guided by a vision—to earn a college degree or motivate/enable someone else to do so, climb a mountain, learn to fly, etc.

ASK participants to write their names in bold letters on the tent cards, fold and set them at their places.

REQUEST that participants briefly introduce themselves by giving their names, where they work, and an example of vision in their lives.

00:05

Overview of the Workshop

REVIEW the workshop, while showing the overhead transparency "A Half-Day Leadership Workshop" on page 191. Flip to the second prepared flipchart "It's Up to You" on page 90 to describe the desired climate of the session. Make these points:

- Vision is often thought of as the touchy-feely part of Leadership training. It is hard to describe because it is personal.

- In the process of describing vision and vision building, we will draw on your experiences, do some interesting activities, and practice some of the skills.

- You are an integral part of what will make this workshop successful. Your active participation is a fundamental requirement to the workshop's success.

00:05

Agenda and Logistics

REVIEW the agenda and logistics, using the overhead "Agenda and Logistics" on page 195. Include the following:

- The topics to be covered, and anticipated completion time.

- The location of restrooms, telephones, smoking areas, etc.

- The arrangements for refreshments, handling messages, etc.

- The necessity for promptness, full participation.

ACKNOWLEDGE that the amount of material to be covered may make you cut off some discussions. Explain that you do this to remain on time and to keep everyone interested.

00:10   **Roles and Responsibilities**

MAKE these points:

- As session facilitator, my role is to guide discussions, facilitate everyone's full involvement, and keep the pace interesting and stimulating.

- Participants' roles are to:
    - Examine and analyze ideas.
    - Test theories and concepts.
    - Practice new skills in a safe environment.

- In doing this you may find that you don't understand someone or something, you disagree with a point, or you want further information. Feel comfortable asking for what you need.

- All of us will practice respect for one another while doing the following:
    - Listening attentively.
    - Not talking when others are.
    - Speaking clearly so that everyone can hear.
    - Returning on time from breaks.

00:30   **Assessment**

REFER to the assessment "Information Gathering (Self)" on page 183.

INTRODUCE the assessment by saying something like:

- Some people absorb information from all around them. Others seem almost deaf and blind, living in their own insulated world.

- In this assessment, answer each question by indicating how often the statement is true of you.

ALLOW 5 to 10 minutes for participants to complete the questionnaire. When most are finished, explain how to score both.

ASK participants to take a moment to assess what this instrument told them about themselves.

REFER to the handout "Openness and Vision" on page 117.

ASK participants to read descriptors of each complete characteristic of openness and autonomy.

ASK participants what they would like to get out of this session, based on their understanding of what will be covered in this session.

NOTE participant requests on a flipchart entitled, "Preferred Emphasis." Include initials of requesters after each one.

POST the flipchart in a prominent space on the wall. You will refer to it later.

 ASK if there are any questions. Answer them as appropriate.

 TRANSITION to the next section, when ready.

2. . . . *Questioning Groupthink (9:00 to 10:15)*

Purpose   This workshop section identifies each person's ability and responsibility to attend to his or her own unique perspective on situations.

Objectives   On completion of this workshop segment, participants will be able to:

- Attend to their perceptions and opinions.

- Identify their values, how these differ from others, and how they shape our decisions.

- Assess their listening skills.

- Know what is involved in acting responsibly toward our insights.

AGENDA: Questioning Groupthink	Minutes 75	Start/Stop 9:00/10:15	Actual Start / Stop	
"Know What We Think" on page 95	10	9:00 / 9:10	_____	_____
"Know What We Value" on page 95	30	9:10 / 9:40	_____	_____
"Act on Our Insights" on page 96	10	9:40 / 9:50	_____	_____
"Listening" on page 97	10	9:50 / 10:00	_____	_____
Break	15	10:00 / 10:15	_____	_____

00:10   **Know What We Think**

ASK participants to turn to the activity entitled "A Few of My Favorite Things" on page 143.

- List five of your favorite pastimes, favorite foods, things you most and least like about work, and things you most and least like about where they live.

TELL participants to follow these guidelines:

- Individually, quickly compile your lists.

- If nothing comes to mind, go to the next list.

- You've got five minutes, so write as fast as you can. Any short-hand you want to use is fine.

CALL TIME after 5 minutes.

DEBRIEF & REVIEW by asking questions such as:

- Those who did not write five items in any of the lists, raise your hands.

- Those who did not write five items in two …(three) …(four) …(five) …(six) of the lists, raise your hands.

- Which categories were most difficult—your *likes* or *dislikes*?

  Most likely, participants will have found positives harder than negatives.

- Would anyone like to hazard a guess as to why these lists might be hard for us?

  The point you want them to reach here is that we don't pay attention to our own opinions and feelings.

- Where do you think this habit of not paying attention to ourselves comes from?

MAKE THE POINT that attending to our responses is crucial to having insight and vision.

00:30   **Know What We Value**

DIRECT participants to work in table groups for the next activity "It's Up to Us to Decide" on page 146.

ASSIGN a case to each table group.

PROVIDE these guidelines from page 145.

- Individually, read the case assigned to your table group.

- When finished, rank the "offenses" described from least accept-able to most acceptable.

- As a group, discuss your perceptions and reach a consensus on the most acceptable item(s).

- Record your responses on a flipchart, keeping your flipchart with its back to the room.

CALL TIME after about 20 minutes.

DEBRIEF & REVIEW the table group discussion by:

- Calling on a spokesperson from each group to report on the case worked on, and the conclusions reached and why.

ASK participants to comment on:

- The ease or difficulty they had in reaching consensus.

- The amount of variability in their group.

- How strongly they felt about the values that were the underpinning for their decisions.

- Their awareness of their attachment to these values prior to the activity.

CONCLUDE by asking participants to list their own values as they became aware of them in this activity.

DISCUSS the activity, using questions such as:

- Do your values—whether you are aware of them or not—influence your decisions and your actions?

- If values are the underlying reasons for our actions, can one change them? Can doing the right thing influence what we value?

- How might a leader use values to influence followers?

00:10   **Act on Our Insights**

MAKE these points:

Leaders tend to have a clearer understanding of what they think and what is important to them. Reasons for this include:

- They pay attention to themselves—their own thoughts and feelings.

- They tend to be more reflective—on what others have to say as well as on what they think and feel.

- They tend to act on what they think and feel.

TELL participants that this is a table group discussion. In a round robin each person should identify the last insight he or she had, and—honestly—how he or she responded to it.

- Have each group appoint a scribe to list on a flip chart all reported insights.

- Call time in 5 minutes.

DEBRIEF the discussion.

00:10   ## Listening

REVIEW this topic by asking questions such as:

- What can you do to improve concentration on what others are saying? You may expect to hear:

  - *Look at the speaker* • *Nod, smile, or look confused* • *Take notes* • *Try to concentrate.*

- What things might hinder your understanding of what others may be saying? You may expect to hear:

  - *Think about something else* • *Look at other people and things* • *Read something else* • *Do other things* • *Plan your next comment.*

- What can you do as a listener that would help the person speaking convey what he/she wants to convey? You may expect to hear:

  - *Ask questions if it isn't clear* • *Verify your understanding* • *Ask the person to sequence, define cause-effect, etc.* • *Respond with your opinion of the speaker's message.*

- Is listening easy or difficult? Answers will vary.

Assessment

REFER to the assessments "Listening Assessment (Self)" on page 173.

INTRODUCE the assessments by saying something like:

- There are different behaviors associated with listening. Some practice none, some, or all of them.

- In these assessment, answer each question by indicating how often the statement is true of you.

ALLOW 5 to 10 minutes for participants to complete the questionnaire. When most are finished, explain how to score both.

ASK participants to take a moment to assess what these instrument told them about themselves.

DIRECT participant attention to the handout "Leaders Learn by Listening" on page 119.

ASK participants what they think creates the greatest challenge to accurate listening.

CONCLUDE by reiterating that effective leaders need to pay close attention to their responses, and those of others.

15:00   **BREAK**

3.... *Develop a Vision (10:15 to 11:55)*

Purpose   This workshop section focuses on developing a personal vision.

Objectives   On completion of this workshop segment, participants will be able to:

- Practice their ability to visualize.

- Identify the need to exercise risk taking if they are to develop and act on vision.

- Communicate a vision.

- Take action to keep the vision alive.

- Identify personal commitments that could develop their autonomy and ability to visualize.

AGENDA: Develop a Vision	Minutes 100	Start/Stop 10:15/11:55	Actual Start / Stop	
"Time Travel—a Visualization" on page 98	20	10:15 / 10:35		
"Risk Taking" on page 100	20	10:35 / 10:55		
"Communicating Your Vision" on page 101	10	10:55 / 11:05		
"Keeping Your Vision Alive" on page 101	30	11:05 / 11:35		
"Commitments" on page 101	10	11:35 / 11:45		
"Recognition Activity" on page 102	10	11:45 / 11:55		

00:20   **Time Travel—a Visualization**

ASK participants to think about one of the things they identified on their list of five *least* favorite things about where they live or work, or a recent insight on which they did not act.

TELL them to close their eyes while you guide them via "Visualization Activity Guidelines" on page 154.

READ this to participants, slowly:

- You are going to do something about this issue that's been hanging.

- What are you going to do about it (pause)?

- Who are you talking to about it (pause)? What are you saying (pause)? What are they saying (pause)? How are you undertaking your project (pause)?

- Fast-forward. It is six months from now. You've taken action. People are giving you credit for what you have done.

- Who are these people?

- Where are you gathered?

- Who is that getting up to recognize you?

- Can you hear what he or she is saying (pause)?

- The voice is describing what you did (pause).

- How you persevered (pause).

- Someone is taking your picture (pause). What are you wearing? How do you look in that picture?

- Someone asks you to tell everyone how you did it (pause).

- You're standing up. You're beginning to tell about the experience (pause).

- You're thanking people who were involved, who supported you (pause)? Who are they?

- How do you feel (pause)?

- How do others feel about you (pause)?

- Now open your eyes.

 ASK participants individually to describe:

- *What* they accomplished.

- *Images* they saw.

- *Feelings* they felt.

- *How others* responded to them.

 REVIEW the activity by asking questions such as:

- What did you visualize?

  Accept a few volunteers.

- Are you more likely to act on this issue now? Why or why not?

  Expect the following: *a few people will say they will now do something about it because of the positive image of the outcome they visualized.*

- When you have visualized taking actions like this in the past, have your visualizations been positive or negative?

  Expect the following: *a few people will say they will now do something about it because of the negative image of the outcome they visualized.*

- How does that affect you?

  Negative visualizations discourage us from taking action.

00:20

Risk Taking

INTRODUCE this activity by making these points:

- One reason we do not act on our insights and dreams is that we visualize *negative consequences*.

- We dwell on the risks—which may be quite real.

- In this table group activity, we're going to choose one risk, that you are discouraged by "we're going to turn it around."

REFER participants to the activity "I Think I Can" on page 157. We will illustrate it using the guidelines for that activity.

TELL participants that for this activity they will work in table groups.

ASK participants if they remember the little train that *could*. Have someone retell the story.

TELL participants that each table is going to construct such a train, powered by their united courage. Each member of the group adds one car to the train.

- Individually, identify the freight you are loading onto your carriage. This "freight" is some risk you would like to take but haven't, because of fear.

- Place "Highly Volatile!" warning signs or other decorations on your rail-car. Color them as time allows.

- As a table, decide what to name your train—e.g., *The Reliability Railway, The Freedom Express, The Courtesy Coaster*, etc.

- Post your train, someplace close to your table. Hitch up your wagons to the engine, and then we'll talk about it.

CALL TIME after 8 to 10 minutes.

NOTE TO FACILITATOR: If your audience is more verbal and less symbolic, you could use "Which One is a Vison" on pages 150-151 instead of the activity above. Guidelines for the activity are on page 149.

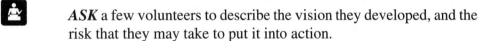

REVIEW the activity by having each table tell the others about their railway and how the "I Think I Can" engine is going to pull their *risk-taking* freight.

00:10

Communicating Your Vision

ASK a few volunteers to describe the vision they developed, and the risk that they may take to put it into action.

HAVE participants read the handout "How to Communicate the Vision" on page 123.

00:30

Keeping Your Vision Alive

INRODUCE group discussion by asking questions such as:

- Why do people forget about a vision, once it has been communicated? Anticipate responses that include:

    ● *Encounter difficulties* ● *Don't see early result* ● *Not enough enthusiasm* ● *No champion* ● *Little encouragement* ● *No owner* ● *etc.*

- What can people do in organizations to keep a vision alive. Anticipate responses such as:

    ● *Take responsibility for cheerleading* ● *Celebrate small successes* ● *Give credit to people who have made an effort* ● *Write article or publish photo in newsletter* ● *Give awards* ● *Recognize efforts* ● *Challenge dissenters* ● *etc.*

NOTE responses on the "Keeping Visions Alive" flipchart.

DEBRIEF the activity as directed in "Leadership Assessment Guidelines" on page 166.

00:10

Commitments

ASK each participant to identify one new insight and one commitment to themselves on the handout "Communicating and Follow-Up" on page 135. While participants are doing this:

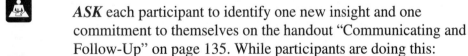

LIST, for each participant, one point for which you can credit them.

00:15   **Recognition Activity**

CALL each participant to come forward and receive his or her "Certificate of Achievement" on page 56.

GIVE participants positive feedback on some aspect of their participation.

ASK others who wish to credit this person to do so while he/she is still at the front of the room.

THANK the group for its participation.

Chapter Six:

One-Hour Leadership Workshop

This *Leadership: ASTD Trainer's Sourcebook* chapter provides a training plan you can use to structure a one-hour leadership workshop. Use it *as is*, or tailor it to your needs. Try running it once or twice as written. Then, based on feedback and experience, modify it to your situation.

This Chapter

… has these parts:

Meeting "Purpose and Objectives" below

Meeting "AGENDA: Giving Credit" on page 104

"Materials Needed" on page 104

"Suggested Flipcharts" on page 105.

Purpose and Objectives

This workshop provides a learning experience focused on *giving credit*—a distinguishing mark of leaders. On completion of the workshop, participants will be able to:

- Identify why and when to give credit (positive feedback).
- Identify opportunities to give credit in their own work settings.
- Give and receive credit.

AGENDA: Giving Credit	Minutes 60	Start/Stop 0:00 / 1:00	Actual Start / Stop	
"The Why and What of "Crediting" " on page 105	15	0:00 / 0:15	_____	_____
"Opportunities for Giving Credit " on page 106	15	0:15 / 0:30	_____	_____
"Giving Credit" on page 106	25	0:30 / 0:55	_____	_____
"Follow-Up" on page 108	5	0:55 / 1:00	_____	_____

Materials Needed

Following are checklists of materials recommended for the one-hour leadership workshop. Masters for these materials are found in Chapters 7, 8, 9, and 10 of this book. Unless otherwise noted:

Make one handout and instrument per participant.

Make one overhead transparency of each one needed.

Prepare one of each flipchart needed.

Handouts

❑ "Giving Positive Feedback" on page 132

Instruments, assessments

Use where indicated:

❑ "Opportunities to Celebrate Successes" on page 186

Learning activities

Use where indicated:

❑ "Giving Credit" on page 163

Overheads

Use where indicated:

❑ "A One-Hour Leadership Workshop" on page 192

❑ "Giving Positive Feedback" on page 194

Suggested Flipcharts

Welcome

to

Giving Credit

**One-Hour Leadership
Training**

Scope

of This Session

- Focus on a single behavioral skill.

- Identify opportunities to use crediting.

- Practice giving credit.

- Personal commitment.

Training Plan

Giving Credit

00:15

The Why and What of "Crediting"

WELCOME participants to the session.

ANNOUNCE the scope of this session., using the "One-Hour Leadership Workshop" overhead on page 192.

MAKE these points:

- This hour focuses on a single skill.

- It concentrates on one used by most leaders, that of giving followers credit for the things that they accomplish in pursuit of the vision.

ASK participants to read the handout "Giving Positive Feedback" on page 132.

TELL participants to read the questions and answer them as honestly as they can.

CALL TIME after 10 minutes.

CALL on volunteers to discuss:

- What did they find out about how well you celebrate successes?

- What difference does celebration of success make?

REVIEW using the overhead "Giving Positive Feedback" on page 194; question participants when they have finished reading.

LEAD A DISCUSSION with participants about why giving credit is important. Anticipate responses such as:

> ● *Encourages people* ● *Motivates people to continue efforts*
> ● *Tells people that what they are doing is important enough to be noticed.*

- Do you frequently receive credit from peers or a superior for what you have accomplished? How does it feel?

  Answers will vary by group.

- Do you frequently give credit to those you work with—superiors, peers, direct reports? Why or why not?

  Answers will vary by group.

00:15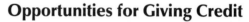

Opportunities for Giving Credit

DIRECT participants to the assessment questionnaire, "Opportunities to Celebrate Successes" on page 186.

TELL participants to read the questions and answer them as honestly as they can.

CALL TIME after 10 minutes.

DEBRIEF the discussion.

CALL on volunteers to respond to questions such as the following:

- What did they find out about how well you celebrate successes?

- What difference does celebration of success make?

ASK participants if this activity has led them to any conclusions about what they want to do with this issue in the future.

00:25   ## Giving Credit

DIRECT participants to the activity handout, "Giving Positive Feedback" on page 132

TELL participants that in this practice activity they will work in pairs.

ASK participants to count off in twos. A *one* and a *two* constitute a working pair.

- Individually, read the directions and prepare your statements and questions.

- *Twos* start the interview by backgrounding *ones*.

- You may improvise in responding to questions.

- Complete the feedback by reaching an agreement.

CALL TIME for feedback at 7 minutes and round two at 10 minutes.

REVIEW the activity by asking questions such as:

- How did it feel to receive feedback?

- How did you feel when you were giving the feedback?

- Is it appropriate to give this type of feedback to peers? to those higher than you in the chain-of-command?

- Where else in your life might you use this skill?

ASK participants to consider why people don't use this skill more. Limit discussion so that the pace is interesting for everyone.

00:05   **Follow-Up**

 ASK participants to estimate how many times in a day they have an opportunity to give credit.

 SUGGEST STRATEGIES that participants may use to remind them of their commitment to giving credit each day. Until it becomes habit, many people use strategies to remind them to give credit daily. You can do things such as:

- Place pennies in the right pocket in the morning, and transfer them one at a time as they credit someone.

- Keep a *crediting* notepad on your desks. At the end of the day, jot a personal note to anyone who you noticed doing the expected during the day.

- Give a credit for every credit that you receive.

- Award yourself a star every time you credit someone.

- Build something, adding a structural element each time you credit someone. Keep it small: e.g., Lego, gingerbread, paper clips.

Chapter Seven:

Participant Handouts

This *Leadership: ASTD Trainer's Sourcebook* chapter provides handouts you can use with the three training designs presented here. If you wish to prepare additional handouts, you may do so by adapting material found in Chapter Two, "Background" starting on page 11, or in any of the resources listed in the *Appendix*. As you expand your knowledge of the topic, you will no doubt modify and add to the core provided here. The readings presented here provide you with the key concepts, theories, and practical applications of the research in the field.

How to Use the Handouts

… some ways you can use these handouts:

As background, in your own preparation for the sessions.

As pre-reading, for participants to read before coming to a session.

As handouts, to read during the session—the option suggested here. (Note that timeframes are tight, however, so in the interest of finding time for additional discussion, you may wish to use either the option above or the one below.)

As handouts, to be read by participants after the session.

Leadership Characteristics

Most people feel they know what leadership is but have a hard time describing it. That is perfectly understandable! We know we understand *what* leadership is because we recognize leaders when we see and hear them. That is because we *agree* with them or we *see* the appeal they have to followers. Perhaps they even *inspire* us. We want to follow. The presence of *followers* is an essential part of being a leader. You can't lead if no one is following!

Since no one can be a leader without *followers*, it is important to know how a leader develops them. He or she captures followers' hopes and dreams and gives them a voice in a vision. Followers are first attracted to the leader when the leader's *vision* resonates in them. The vision may address wrongs they care about, and it may cast the possible solution in *worthy* or even *heroic* terms. Achieving the future that followers care about is portrayed as a noble pursuit. This vision conforms to their values, hence its attraction.

Followers may become attached to the leader at any phase of the mission. Some join when they hear about the vision. Their commitment may come while working with the leader on projects related to the vision. They may be inspired by the example of people committed to the vision. As a committed core of followers forms, it attracts more people.

The root of the word *lead* means "to go." A *leader's vision* takes followers somewhere. We think of leaders as people with a mission, pioneers who inspire and encourage, often leading us to accomplish our personal best. They are motivated. Usually they have strongly held principles, which guide their actions. Being goal-oriented and principle-centered, they are agile in adjusting tactics to accommodate unforeseen obstacles that block them. How they get to the goal is not as important as the goal itself.

Leader Practices

Leaders are characterized by a number of distinctive practices. All of these descriptions have common themes—*openness to change, ability to visualize the future, be guided by a vision and communicate it powerfully to others, entrust the mission to others, display commitment through action,* and *encourage followers*. Here are the leadership categories. Writers about leadership agree on a core set of characteristics which they call by different names. Most agree on the names of the five characteristics given here:

Characteristic #1—Question Groupthink **by:**

- Being curious—investigating, asking "why," asking questions, listening, verifying understanding, reflecting

- Taking initiative, risks, experimenting

- Being open to diverse opinions

- Encouraging creativity, innovation

Characteristic #2—Reset Direction **by:**

- Developing a vision—synthesizing recurring themes and values

- "Selling" the vision—presenting a compelling vision of a possible future

- Enlisting others—asking for help, showing how they can make a difference

Characteristic #3—Guide Cooperative Action **by:**

- Planning, setting team goals

- Empowering followers

- Encouraging initiative

- Delegating authority

- Coaching, monitoring

- Providing constructive feedback

Characteristic #4—Walk the Talk **by:**

- Involvement—setting an example of personal commitment

- Committing to quality outcomes

- Helping solve problems

- Being persistent

Characteristic #5—Motivate Others **by:**

- Recognizing individual and team contributions

- Giving positive feedback

- Celebrating accomplishments

- Reinforcing teamwork

Notes:

_____

_____

_____

A Leader I've Known

All of us have known leaders. Some of them are introduced to us through the media, because of a heroic deed or an extraordinary lifetime of dedication. Names such as Martin Luther King or Mother Teresa may come to mind. Leadership does not have to be so heroic, however. It is all around us. No doubt you've known someone who dedicated a life to something. This person probably loved what they were doing, enjoyed talking about it, and built enthusiasm in others. The person probably spent a lot of time on this passion, and in the process probably touched many lives. Who was this person, and how did he or she demonstrate leadership characteristics?

Notes:

_____

_____

_____

_____

_____

_____

_____

_____

_____

_____

_____

_____

_____

_____

Recognizing Leadership

Since followership is an essential part of being a leader, we are all qualified to identify people we would follow. When we look at these, we can identify that they have *many* or all of the characteristics we have described. In fact, if they lack some of these, it may be the reason why they are not as powerful a leader as they might have been.

Look at the excerpt on "Ghandi" below. From the synopsis of this leader's life, can you identify each of the characteristics identified by authorities on leadership?

Mohandas Karachand Ghandi led his nation to independence of British rule through a campaign of nonviolence that lasted most of his life. Educated in law, at University College, London, he was admitted to the British bar in 1891. Returning home to Bombay, he was unable to get a job. Eventually he was hired by a firm with offices in Durban, South Africa—where he lived the next 20 years. Here, he found himself treated as a member of an inferior race, which became the catalyst for his struggle for Indian rights.

Influenced by Henry David Thoreau's essay, "Civil Disobedience," Gandhi began to campaign for Indian rights and to practice a form of civil disobedience called *satyagraha (truth and firmness)*. By 1914 the South African government had made concessions to his demands for recognition of Indian marriages and abolition of the poll tax. He returned to India to campaign for home rule.

There, he launched a campaign of passive resistance to Great Britain. He gained millions of followers. When British soldiers massacred Indians demonstrating against use of emergency powers, Gandhi organized a campaign of noncooperation. Indians holding public office resigned. Indians boycotted schools and courts. People blocked streets by refusing to move. They boycotted British goods. Gandhi championed the revival of cottage industry, and, as a token of the return to the simple village life he preached, began using a spinning wheel.

Gandhi became the symbol of a free India. He lived a spiritual and ascetic life, fasting and meditating. His advocacy of nonviolence was an expression of Hindu belief. Until his death in 1948 (by a Hindu fanatic—who *didn't* practice nonviolence), Gandhi faced imprisonment numerous times. He fasted frequently, one of his nonviolent weapons. These fasts were effective against the British, who feared violent revolution should he die. He became known as *Mahatma (*great soul), a title reserved for sages. He tried many times to withdraw from politics, but the people looked to him for guidance as the British granted limited home rule, then partitioned the country into India and Pakistan and granted independence.

Question Groupthink

_____

_____

_____

_____

Reset Direction

_____

_____

_____

_____

Guide Cooperative Action

_____

_____

_____

_____

Walk the Talk

_____

_____

_____

_____

Motivate Others

_____

_____

_____

_____

Types of Leaders

When we think of leadership characteristics we might assume they are found only in democratic environments, that all leaders espouse values we admire, or that the characteristics which seem so appealing in the abstract are always admirable. Not so! History tells us that is not the case. Leaders come in all personality types. They espouse a spectrum of values, are found in all cultures, and are at once *products* of those environments and their *architects*. Writers describe these differences in leadership types in different ways—after one set of ancient gods or another. Other writers describe them in more common cultural terms. The following, highly simplified synopsis owes its genesis to three sources, Sandra Krebs Hirsh and Jean M. Kummerow,[1] William Schneider,[2] and Charles Hand.

- *HIGH CONTROL* environments both attract and nurture leaders who are more inclined to be *traditional, stabilizing forces*. These leaders work from a strong sense of responsibility, loyalty, and industry. They tend to be excellent in environments that require disciplined processes and timely output. Such leaders are more controlling.

- *HIGHLY CHALLENGING* or *volatile* environments, attract and advance leaders with a bent for *troubleshooting, negotiating*, and *firefighting*. Such leaders may be bored by the routine but are challenged by the unexpected. Such leaders need to constantly "raise the bar." They are highly innovative.

- Environments that *VALUE IDEAS* and *PERSONAL VALUES* attract and develop leaders whose temperament is energized by *introspection* and *interaction* with people. Such leaders are moved by a personal sense of possibilities and a strong sense of mission. These leaders are inspiring.

- *ENTREPRENEURIAL* environments attract and encourage leaders with a strong *strategic sense*. These leaders combine creativity and ingenuity with logic. They are courageous and strategic.

We are usually attracted to work environments that match our temperaments, just as we respond to *leaders* who are like ourselves.

---

1   *Introduction to Type in Organizations*, 2nd edition, Palo Alto, Consulting Psychologist Press, Inc., 1990
2   *The Reengineering Alternative: Making Your Corporate Culture Work for You*, New York, Irwin One, 1994

Management and Leadership

It's now time to refine our understanding of leadership in the context of management. Many people who are *managers* are also *leaders*. But a manager does *not* have to be a leader. Likewise, many people who are *leaders* would be much more effective if they practiced good management techniques.

Below is a list of characteristics and practices. Each one is integral to the definition of one or the other. In other words, we will not focus here on the areas that may overlap in any one individual. Rather we want to identify those characteristics or practices that belong within the classic definition of *either* management or leadership:

1. *Plans* for the future.

2. *Sees the future*, and makes plans to attain it.

3. Empowers others, *encourages decision making*.

4. Encourages *risk taking*.

5. Monitors *workforce uniformity*, according to known procedures and standards.

6. *Minimizes risk*, by taking cautious, proven courses of action.

7. Builds around *rules*.

8. Builds around *values*.

9. Controls *change* and *evolution*.

10. Strives to make *change* happen.

11. Matches *assistance* to the need of the individual.

12. Relies on *structured hierarchy* to denote authority and power.

13. Relies on *referent* (freely given allegiance) *power base*.

14. *Investigates* and *discusses* diverse ideas openly.

15. Confines discussion to *current problems* and options.

16. Uses position to *reward* or *coerce action*.

17. Investigates personal strengths and *matches strengths* to *needs*.

18. *Focuses* on *people* as an essential part of attaining the outcome—product or service.

Openness and Vision

Curiosity and *openness* is the root of the leader's questioning the status quo and building the vision of a better future.

Curiosity

Leaders tend to have wide interests. They ask a lot of questions, particularly *why*. Their questioning is not fault finding. Leaders are good listeners because they are genuinely interested in hearing what others have to say. They hear what customers and co-workers suggest or request.

When they recognize *inconsistencies, inefficiencies,* and *un-met needs* they note it. When input combines into a clear message, a *vision* emerges. This insight is unique to the leaders.

This is not to say that all leader insights are valid. Many are not. When an insight proves unfeasible, improbable, or unworkable, the leader discards it. An important mark of a leader is that he or she is not afraid to test insights and find them wanting. In these early stages, leaders are as open to challenges as they are to challenging others. This open discussion helps them focus on the essentials of what is wrong with the current approach and why it should be changed, and what pursuing the vision could accomplish.

Openness

Leaders are more apt to "think outside the box" (referring to the solution to the puzzle whose nine-dots you connect with four straight lines), to try new and unproved methods to get to the goal. They are less likely to defend the status quo, and more likely to listen to challenging ideas. This openness results in their willingness to champion team efforts that cut steps, time, or effort from a function, to look at different approaches and new technologies—in other words to lead change.

Paradigm blindness

The great enemy of openness is not an unwillingness to see things from the point of view of others, but the inability to do so. This is called, by Joel Barker *paradigm blindness*. Barker describes this phenomenon as the tendency to perceive what we expect to, and the inability to notice or take seriously phenomena outside our expectations. For examples he cites xerography and the quartz watch, inventions which challenged and were ignored or rejected by those to whom they were shown.

Conventional thinking

A reason for paradigm blindness is overuse of a very useful learning tool—generalizing. One of the great advantages we humans have in learning is our ability to generalize. We intuit a rule from several examples and apply that rule to all instances of that class. This ability to generalize—to organize experience, see patterns, relationships, underlying laws—helps us integrate new knowledge and is an essential leadership trait, used for developing vision.

Overgeneralizing

However, a rule can be over applied. We call that *over-generalizing*. We all do this at times—failing to realize that a rule which applies most of the time has exceptions. Or that there are other generalizations which are equally valid, even if we do not yet know them. We sometimes refer to overgeneralizing as *stereotyping* or the result as having a *mindset*. Both have negative connotations, indicating a lack of openness and fair-mindedness. Overgeneralizing is damaging when it leads us to treat people or ideas only as part of a category. It leads us to disregard the unique traits of events.

Fear

Another opponent of openness is fear. Most of us have some fear of the unknown. That fear is the basis of predictions of dire consequences of change—consequences include the loss of cherished values, fear of economic consequences, or fear of inability to learn the new ways of doing things.

Initiative

Unlike dreamers, leaders test their ideas in action. When they reject ideas they don't see this as failure. They have a type of courage, an ability to maintain a positive outlook when things don't work out. They are also able to handle change and high amounts of stress, a quality referred to in the literature as *psychological hardiness* or *resistance*.

Leaders Learn by Listening

Leaders learn a lot about what people think, what is important to them, because they listen. The hallmarks of their listening includes:

Aspects of a Good Listener

Accessible	Available when people want to talk.
Interested	Eager to know what other people think and feel.
Attentive	Concentrates on the person speaking.
Encourages expression	Encourages others to say what they really feel and think.
Doesn't interrupt	Listens without the need to offer other viewpoints.
Suspends judgment	Makes no decision until all viewpoints have been heard.
Values different views	Respects different viewpoints.
Shows empathy and understanding	Demonstrates empathy through action and understanding through verifying.
Doesn't talk too much	Does not seek to dominate conversation.

Accessible

Many busy managers close their doors so they can complete paperwork. Others find that they end up doing the paperwork before others arrive in the morning or after they leave for the day—because they are always accessible to those who want to drop in to consult them or to those who want to reach them by telephone. Followers know the person is *accessible*.

Interested

People who are really interested in what another has to say ask questions, want to know details, and explore avenues that the person talking might not have thought about. Interested listeners are valuable.

Attentive

One sign of interest is the way the listener *attends* to the speaker. Signs of attention include looking at the person, taking notes, and following what is said.

Encourages expression

Sometimes it is necessary to coax people to speak up, to share thoughts. There are those who think their thoughts are insignificant, or that no one cares. Leaders tend to encourage expression of views by asking lots of questions. They solicit input more widely by encouraging use of suggestion boxes, open door policies, and informal gatherings where everyone mingles on an equal footing.

Doesn't interrupt

Letting someone finish a thought—even a rambling one you have heard umpteen times before—reinforces an image of *interest*. It is, of course, also a mark of respect and courtesy practiced in most civil discourse.

Suspends judgment

One reason why good listeners don't interrupt is because they are willing to suspend judgment until they have heard the whole story.

Values different views

A leader's source for views is often his or her ability to synthesize widely varying opinions by finding common concerns in them.

Shows empathy, understanding

Leaders have a variety of ways of showing they have heard what speakers are telling them. Verifying understanding is an obvious way. Taking action on what has been explained is another. Action that demonstrates empathy may take the form of food and toy drives, actions to assist with medical care or assistance in a catastrophe.

Doesn't talk too much

Though a leader may speak eloquently, he or she will know *how* and *when* to be quiet.

Notes to Self

Based on what you learned about yourself, how do you want to improve your listening skills?

_____

_____

_____

_____

How Vision Develops

There is nothing mystical about vision. Neither is it commonplace. It is not the result of analytical thought alone—it also requires insight and intuition. The word vision connotes:

- A vivid image.

- An ideal or standard of excellence.

- A future orientation or desired destination.

What is vision?

Many prefer to use other words—such as *goal, mission, objective, calling,* or *personal agenda* instead of *vision.* Whatever its name, vision is a vivid "picture" of both a future destination and the journey along the way. It is rich in detail and feeling—you know what it will look or sound like, and how it will feel, what it will be like to reach the destination. This image provides a focus and a context for the efforts of a leader and his or her followers. Such a vision is consistent with the larger context of our lives—our values, our personal strengths, our experiences, and, within an organization, its overall mission or overriding challenge.

Developing a vision

Developing this image requires creativity. Many of us left this part of ourselves in kindergarten—or possibly would not admit to not having done so. But all of us have the ability to create a vision.

Developing a vision involves becoming immersed enough with the topic that it thoroughly engages the mind. This means that we develop visions about the things in which we are already involved. That involvement must be mental as well as physical. The vision often starts with a persistent problem. Or it may start with formal planning activities—breaking the achievement of the desired outcome into components, and putting timeframes to them. Others induce this state by reading and discussion.

Once the mind engages the prospect, it starts developing scenarios. Small snatches of what might happen become vivid images. John Robinson, in his book *Coach to Coach* discusses this process in detail. He likens it to daydreaming. He also points out that the imagination becomes most active with these images when the leader pulls back from the hands-on activities into what he describes as *30-second sabbaticals.*

A vivid image is really the repository of a lot of information. It is useful to the leader on the journey toward the goal, who tests possible scenarios against it and answers questions by consulting it.

**How we build
a vision**

Everyone's personal vision for the future derives from:

- Past experiences.

- Personal values.

- Listening to others—co-workers, customers, suppliers.

- Reflection—one's own intuition, ability to make connections and to generalize.

**Visions grow
when shared**

The way to clarify a vision is to discuss it with others—friends, co-workers, anyone who will listen. What started as a vague notion will either become more vivid and compelling or will fizzle out. It's as if discussing it and acting on it brings the distant image closer and makes it more focused.

**Influence
of the past**

When building a vision, we use our *organizational* and *industry experience*, as well as *past accomplishments* and *mistakes*. By first looking at our past, experts indicate that we develop a longer time horizon and richer detail when envisioning the future. The more varied the experience and the input we've gathered, the more possibilities we see in current situations.

**Why visions
attract**

Experience, desire, reflection, imagination, insight, and *intuition* combine forces. The result is a unique spin on a current situation that challenges by asking "why not?" The vision is known with certainty to be possible, "if only…." This challenge to action is a defining characteristic of vision, separating it from dreams. In challenging others to achieve that possibility, leaders show others how attractive the future could be with their efforts. This view often resonates with followers because it reflects their input and articulates their own views and secret desires.

Notes:

_____

_____

_____

_____

_____

How to Communicate the Vision

Once a vision is vividly perceived, a leader must be able to communicate it. Leaders feel the need to communicate their vision because they believe in it, feel strongly about it, and are compelled to act on it. To communicate it effectively, the leader must be able to present ideas effectively. Here are pointers for preparing a compelling vision presentation:

Prepare a vision statement

To prepare a vision statement the leader must:

- Prepare a *clear, concise statement of the vision.* It should take no longer than five minutes to present. Aim for *logic, clarity,* and *simplicity.*

- Find *examples* that illustrate the central point. These may be *heroic*, such as a well-known historic event; *local* such as an event all are familiar with; or of *human interest* (appeal to the heart). Integrate these illustrations into the message.

- Discover one or two *metaphors* that illustrate the vision. This should be something people can relate to, and that helps you make your point vividly or humorously.

- Identify *a key phrase.* Is there a key phrase that you might use as a refrain? Is there a line of poetry, a line from a song, hymn, or historic document that resonates with the idea you are describing? Integrate quotations and key phrases into your presentation.

- *Practice* the presentation and adjust it until you are *comfortable* with it. You are comfortable when you enter into the feeling of what you want to convey and forget the tension of speaking.

Repeat vision

Once communicated, a leader never lets the team forget. John Kotter cites under-communication of the vision as a prime reason why some visions fail. The leader who reinforces the message, uses every available vehicle to do so! Possibilities include:

- Reviewing the message in frequent pep talks.

- Using phrases as slogans for activities, contests, etc.

- Referring back to it during meetings and recognition events.

- Placing team members' roles in the context of attaining the vision when discussing their areas of responsibility.

- Tying it to the overall goal of the organization.

- Making posters for key phrases and posting them in prominent places.

- Making medallions, coins, or plaques that remind individuals of their importance in a larger context.

- Using a key phrase to name a newsletter or other internal communication device.

- Writing editorials on key aspects of the vision.

- Recognizing and rewarding behavior that furthers the vision.

Notes:

_____

_____

_____

_____

_____

_____

_____

_____

_____

_____

_____

_____

_____

_____

_____

_____

_____

Roles and Responsibilities

Where the vision requires a team

In organizing any effort to pursue a goal, you must identify what has to happen to achieve it. Large endeavors usually require more than one individual—which involves dividing the tasks. Still larger endeavors require several people assigned to define aspects of the task, which leads to the requirement to formalize who is responsible for what, and to list the tasks for which each is responsible. In good teams, there is also some measurement of what it means to successfully accomplish the role's outcomes. This is all part of planning.[1]

What often happens in mature operations is that roles become highly analyzed and codified to salary schedules. The tasks and responsibilities assigned to them become solidified, and it may take ingenuity on the part of the leader to alter them or to circumvent the tangle of bureaucracy.

Define skill requirements

The important thing about assigning roles and responsibilities is to define clearly what skills and talents each role needs, then find the people who have those skills and talents. People may have limitations or talents that cross role boundaries. In such cases, creative leaders are inclined to restructure responsibilities, so that they can avail themselves of the best each has to offer.

Strengths are motive source

It makes sense to tailor roles and responsibilities to the strengths of team members. People are usually good at the things for which they have talent. They learn it easily. They like doing it, and usually have an interest in excelling at it. They do not need external motivation. They will happily stay involved with it for long stretches of time, because it is rewarding to them.

Similarly, people avoid that which they do not do well, what they have no talent for and where learning mastery comes with difficulty. These are the aspects of jobs that they neglect or put off until there is no longer any way to avoid them.

Responsibility sharing

Even where the organization does not permit restructuring of job responsibilities, workers often strike deals with peers. One may enjoy a role another may detest. They may trade responsibilities. Such approaches allow one to benefit from the individual strengths and intrinsic motivation of all the players.

---

1   See *Supervision*: *The ASTD Trainer's Sourcebook*, by Bobette Hays Williamson, for more on this topic.

Tailor Your Coaching

Ken Blanchard and Paul Hersey's advice on tailoring coaching to the needs of individuals makes rational sense and provides the would-be coach with a simple heuristic to tailoring intervention with each team member. (The application of that heuristic may not be so simple, however!) We all acknowledge that a swimmer who knows the basics would be wasting time getting drills in basic techniques. It would be equally foolish to throw someone into the deep end of the pool under the assumption that given the opportunity, they will spontaneously know how to swim. Leaders tailor their coaching to an individual's current level in these areas:

1. **Skill**—Is this person a *novice* or a *master,* or *somewhere in between*? People learn skills easily if they have an aptitude for that area. Don Clifton and Paula Nelson call this trait, "easy learning."[1]

2. **Experience**—The person may have well-developed skills, but never before used them in this setting. Or the person may have a lot of experience, but all the needed skills may not be developed. A case in point would be hiring someone from a certain industry to sell to that industry, even though he has not sold before. The hiring organization may feel that they can teach the selling skills and product knowledge, but could not teach the industry knowledge that experience in the industry imparts.

3. **Motivation**—Frequently people who have both skill and experience in an area become bored with it. It doesn't challenge them any more. They may feel that to continue means they are not promotable. So they feel *washed up burned out*—in a word, *demotivated*. Such people may have lots of talent and great experience. But that is past. Such people challenge the leader to reignite the fire of interest.

Because roles and responsibilities usually include a complex of requirements, the same individual may vary on these three dimensions across a number of the requirements. A salesperson who is good at prospecting on the telephone, may be terrible in putting written proposals together—both responsibilities of the sales role. This is part of what makes tailoring your coaching a challenge. For each team member complete a chart, identify key responsibilities on one side, and check their level—*high, medium, low*—for the three areas.

---

1   Don O. Clifton and Paula Nelson, *Soar on Your Strengths.*

Coaching Worksheet

Name: _____

Responsibilities	Skill Level	Motivation	Experience

Coaching Notes:

_____

_____

_____

_____

_____

_____

_____

_____

_____

_____

_____

_____

_____

Training the Team

The best organizations pay attention to mastery of the basics. They do not ask people to do something for which they have not been given the tools and training. Like coaching, this is tailored to individual needs and responsibilities. As in role assignment and coaching, it involves analysis of the *team members* and the *vision*.

Based on needed results

Analyze the skills and knowledge needed for each role. Identify the knowledge needed for each position, and see that everyone has easy access to it. If the knowledge resides in someone's head, a helpline to that person must be set up. If the knowledge is online, on CD-ROM, microfiche, database, even print, workers need training in how to access it.

Skills training is often easier. In addition to offering formal training sessions, many organizations pair experienced and inexperienced workers. New workers are assigned to their trainer long enough for them to see how that person handles all aspects of the job. Others assign mentors to the partially experienced, so that they have a personal guide who can advise them as they encounter challenges.

Scorekeeping

Most people are more involved in their functions if there is some type of scorekeeping. In football, that involves statistics as well as game outcomes. Statistics help identify how well the basics were employed. These are advance indicators of likely outcomes. The actual score tells the outcome, and involves things such as luck, penalties, etc. Quality conscious organizations institute both types of scorekeeping. These standards and outcome expectations are well known to the players, who are involved in their tracking and analysis. These outcomes tell the team and the leader how much additional training and coaching is needed.

Realistic standards

In keeping score, a leader knows that the ideal may not be feasible without a lot of growth and additional training. For example, we do not ask Little League players to perform on a World Series level. But we often have equivalent expectations of team efforts in other environments. This is the fallacy that if we set standards they are achievable. The ideal must be set and progress toward it measured. Then the gap between it and what is currently possible must be measured. Only then do we set the realistic standards and the progress that is desired. Making that progress must involve training, tools, and "people power."

Autonomy and Control

Achieving the right balance of autonomy and control is often a problem for the leader. There are some environments where quality controls are of the utmost priority.

Need for controls

In many instances, compliance with controls is a good thing. None of us would want drug manufacturers to haphazardly manufacture medicines. We all feel glad that aircraft pilots are disciplined in completing pre-flight checks. These represent situations where consistency and zero defects are important to our well-being.

Autonomy

At other times, *autonomy* is also a good thing. By autonomy we mean the expectation that someone will freely decide on the correct course of action. If the person chooses to consult with another that decision is his or her own.

The two coexist

Autonomy and *controls* may exist in the same environments, and frequently do. For example, the surgeon who follows rigorous protocols in the operating room, must exercise autonomy when deciding that operating is the course of action to follow. The pilot who completes an extensive pre-flight checklist must exercise autonomy when encountering a storm or malfunction.

Achieving balance

The key in most environments is distinguishing where to institute controls and where to put reliance on the individual problem-solving skills of the people handling the problems. The *Harvard Business Review* series on the *Lifetime Value of Customers* and the *Service-Profit Chain* gives numerous examples of excellent service organizations where frontline workers are given broad authority to take actions that ensure customer satisfaction.

Examples

At British Airways, customer service representatives may quickly take the actions necessary to remedy situations that cause customer dissatisfaction. Hyatt Hotels give frontline employees the ability to take action that represents significant cash value to remedy dissatisfaction. Such instances result in employees feeling a greater sense of responsibility for achieving the common vision.

The key

Leaders who value the involvement of their people are careful to identify where initiative and autonomy are desirable and appropriate. They do not fall into the trap of overgeneralizing that because controls are needed in some areas they must apply to all.

Motivating the Team

Motivating others is the last leadership characteristic. This, like the others, is a multifaceted process. Fundamental to it is an understanding of what motivates people. Much of what has been written about motivation in management literature focuses on attitudes towards people and what motivates them. Another approach is to look at what is intrinsically motivating to someone, and what is extrinsically motivating to them.

Intrinsic and Extrinsic Motivation

Intrinsic rewards

Something is intrinsically motivating, when it provides its own reward. Someone who is dedicated to improving his craft—of sales, music, or carpentry—experiences a thrill in taking that craft to a new level of skill. Such people find great satisfaction in finishing a long or difficult process, even though there may not be recognition by others. A writer who achieves a new level in writing a manuscript, a salesperson who executes a sales process with greater finesse than ever before, a craftsperson who executes an intricate piece of work, all experience a thrill in executing their craft skillfully. We call this *intrinsic* motivation. The writer Mihialy Csikszentimihalyi calls it the experience of *flow*.[1] People tend to repeat those experiences.

You've often heard these people say, "I can't believe that people pay me for doing this. I'm having so much fun." They have discovered the intrinsic reward in what they do. This is why it is important for leaders to learn people's strengths, to know how they like to work, and to provide the preferred level of coaching or independence.

Extrinsic rewards

People also experience feedback from others for what they do. This feedback is *extrinsic*. Rewarding feedback may be the recognition that results from completing tasks that are significant to others. The publication of the finished book and positive book reviews are extrinsic rewards to the writer. Recognition events for achieving milestones are extrinsic motivation to workers on long projects. For some people, especially those who are extroverted, these rewards are especially important.

Extrinsic rewards are also important for teams, because they serve to bond the group in the experience of having accomplished something together.

---

1   Mihaly Csikszentimihalyi, *Flow: The Psychology of Optimal Experience,* New York: Harper & Row, 1990.

Encouraging the Individual Team Member

Intrinsic motivators

Encouragement starts with each individual. Leaders start by taking the easy way—assigning people to aspects of the vision that they are best at, providing them with the training to be successful, giving them enough challenge to keep it interesting, and keeping score, so that the individual knows his success level and can gain satisfaction from it.

Team members also derive satisfaction from the knowledge that they are engaged in an endeavor that has meaning beyond their own small contribution. Being constantly reminded of the goal encourages many to persist when they might otherwise give up. Likewise the camaraderie they share with team members provides reassurance and support.

Because leaders tend to *know* people in general and their followers in particular, they tend to know what motivates them, how they like to work, their skill, motivation, and confidence levels. Because leaders tend to like their followers, they often refer to them as family. They create ways to foster openness and to get to know people on a personal level. They are involved with and in touch with them. They know their aspirations and dreams. That knowledge is invaluable when providing extrinsic recognition.

Giving credit

Credit—providing positive feedback—is one of the most motivating of extrinsic motivators. In crediting individual performance, leaders are careful to be credible. A credible source is one who demonstrates a knowledge of the specifics of an event and can describe the significance of the event in the context of a larger picture. No matter how autonomous or empowered the worker, everyone likes to know that what they are doing is being noticed and appreciated by someone.

Leaders give credit on a regular and frequent basis. They recognize the ordinary and extraordinary efforts people make. They tend to be appreciative of small acts of thoughtfulness. They privately or publicly credit team members as often as opportunity permits.

They also recognize unfruitful effort and risk taking—even when these efforts do not produce the desired results. Reinforcing risk taking, innovation, and honest effort that fails is as important as reinforcing the efforts that end in the desired results. From a motivation standpoint, workers when successful, get intrinsic rewards from the task. The failed exploit, on the other hand, has a built-in negative reinforcement.

In addition to crediting risk taking and failed effort, the leader helps identify the lessons learned from the unfruitful effort.

Giving Positive Feedback

Crediting steps

Here is how to give credible credit:

1 *Identify* the result the person achieved.

2 *Note* one or two elements about the behavior that were critical to achieving that result.

3 *Explain* why that result was important to the mission of the group.

4 *Offer* your appreciation.

Why be so structured?

There are reasons for each step. The first acknowledges the person's performance and clearly identifies that you are aware of it. Next comes the credibility builder—the part that the leader who is "out and about" among his group has no problem with. It requires that you know what the person did, the risk he or she took, the effort required, the problems encountered—in other words the real details. Tying the performance to the greater significance of the group's vision identifies the importance of the action—which is something the person may not have thought about. Then comes the *thank you*.

When to credit

Credit should especially be given for *effort* and *risk taking*—even when the desired results are not achieved. Credit at such times should be coupled with constructive feedback and support in problem solving. This support involves teaching how to analyze failures (before memory fades) to learn valuable lessons. The leader should publicly credit team members when opportunities arise.

Leaders are generous with credible crediting! It is a reason why their followers are willing to make *great effort* for them.

Notes:

_____

_____

_____

_____

_____

_____

_____

_____

Giving Constructive Feedback

Standards

Leaders know that high expectations are motivating. They also know that there is nothing more de-motivating than one or two team members who bring down the level or results for the whole team. In a sports setting, such performance might cost the team *ranking* or a *game*. In a business setting, it may put pressure on other team members, or result in failure to meet quality standards or timeframes.

Usually, team members will monitor from within. However, it is the responsibility of the leader to make sure that constructive feedback is given when it is required—not withstanding the training and coaching that is on-going.

Team membership requires performance levels. Members are responsible for maintaining them.

Constructive feedback steps

To give constructive feedback, a leader must:

1   Make a direct statement indicating what the behavior or performance level is and why its a problem.

2   Ask the person to comment on what is causing this behavior.

3   Discuss (back and forth) the consequences of the behavior performance level continuing at it's current level.

4   Ask the person to identify what he or she can do to change the behavior. Set levels and timeframes.

5   Agree to next steps, and a review date.

Notes:

_____

_____

_____

_____

_____

_____

_____

_____

Opportunities to Celebrate Success

We is a telltale word for the leader. The leader plans with the team. Team members own the process. By tapping into the leadership qualities in the team, the leader creates an atmosphere of appropriate challenge, recognition for achievement, and support for risk taking. Team members are challenged to use judgment, to take calculated risks, and to learn from their own mistakes. In a nurturing team environment, "mistakes" are a natural outcome of making decisions. The important thing the team learns from them is to correct them quickly.

Providing the environment that nurtures this type of involvement and ownership is critical to a team spirit.

Building camaraderie

Some leaders have institutionalized occasions to credit team efforts and build team bonds. These include:

- Friday afternoon beer bashes, such as those favored by some Silicon Valley companies.

- Rankless gatherings such as the weekly "holy hour" favored in some of the British armed forces. Here anybody can say anything that is on his or her mind to any other member of the fraternity, regardless of rank. After "holy hour," such fluid lines of communication evaporate.

- Casual days. Casual dress is a metaphor for the lifting of barriers to communications.

- Organization recreational events such as picnics, outings, sports teams.

- Organizational recognition celebrations, and roasts.

- Organization-sponsored community service events including week-end clean-up projects, sponsorship of school or sporting events.

These activities tend to raise spirits and lower inhibitions, such as fostering closeness, camaraderie, and trust.

Recognize contributions

Extrinsic rewards are also important to member-standing within the team. These can take many forms: a public thank you, monetary incentives, plaques, special parking spaces, etc. It is wise to keep extrinsic rewards simple, so that they do not overshadow or displace the intrinsic reward the person gets from doing the task.

Commitment and Follow-Up

1   I have gained these insights from this training session which I intend to act upon in the future:

_____

_____

_____

_____

_____

_____

_____

_____

_____

2   In the next four weeks I intend to put these practices into effect:

_____

_____

_____

_____

_____

_____

_____

_____

_____

_____

Notes

_____

_____

_____

_____

_____

_____

_____

_____

_____

_____

_____

_____

_____

Chapter Eight:

Learning Activities

This *Leadership: ASTD Trainer's Sourcebook* chapter provides you with facilitated *leading* activities for use in your workshops. Most of these *activities* are used in one of the learning designs. They are a major vehicle for integrating the content of the workshops with the learner's personal experiences and skills. As with all other materials in this sourcebook, you can use the activities *as is*, or you can tailor them to your audience. Again the advice is to run them first *as written*. Then, based on feedback from the sessions and your experience, modify them to your situation.

How to Use the Activities

… among the ways of using these activities:

As part of one of the training designs provided in this book

As a stand-alone activity, to illustrate a specific point or stimulate discussion

Together with a related handout to provide a short training or review session

As part of another training session which covers similar points

As part of your routine meetings with a group.

Chapter structure

Each activity in this chapter contains these elements:

- Objective
- Time required
- Materials you will need
- Procedure
- Alternatives (if appropriate)

Life Path Activity Guidelines

Objective(s)   This activity opens participants to visualizing by:

- Encouraging visual recollections of past experiences.

- Provoking thinking about the future. (Many believe our ability to see into the future is stimulated by our recollection of our past.)

- Proving that all of us *do* create visions, and *can visualize*.

Time   15 minutes.

Material   In addition to the handout on the next page, it is good to provide these materials for each table:

- A large pack of fine point markers in rainbow colors.

- Alternatively, a can of sharpened pencils of various colors.

Procedure

TELL participants to do the following on copies of "Life Path" on page 139:

- Draw an *X* at the point where you are now on this highway.

- Draw five representations—icons, symbols, road signs, billboards—of your major life influences. Influences can include events, relationships, responsibilities, etc.

- Denote five more upcoming attractions on your journey. The attractions do not have to be major, or far in the future, merely something you dream about or wish for.

CALL TIME after about 8-10 minutes.

TELL participants to share their illustrations within their table groups. Allow about 5 minutes.

Debrief

REVIEW the table group discussion by asking questions such as:

- Were you able to identify five images from your future?

- How far into the future did you go?

- Would you agree that you can visualize some things in your life? How would you describe the things that you can visualize?

You're looking for responses such as—things that are personally important, we find attractive, make us feel good.

Life Path

The following picture depicts the path, road, highway, of your life. Notice that the landscape has no details. You must provide those.

1   Draw an X on the road where you are in your life.

2   Create at least five drawings illustrating major experiences in your life to now. They can be signposts, billboards, topographical features (mountains, rivers, or other terrain you've crossed) or representations of meaningful relationships or experiences.

3   Illustrate at least five major attractions on the road ahead of you.

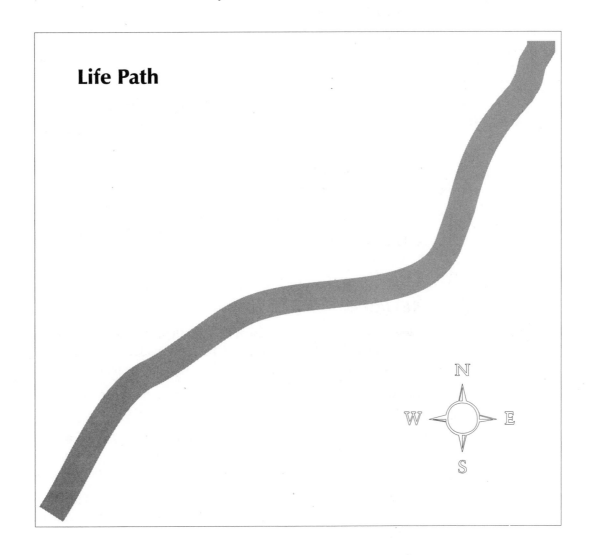

Life Path

Figures of Speech Activity Guidelines

Objective(s) This activity alerts participants to these facts:

- Figures of speech are commonly used in everyday life.

- They enhance the vividness of communication.

Time 10 minutes.

Materials For this activity these supplies are recommended in addition to "Images Are Everywhere" on page 141.

Flipchart for each table group or group of 4-6 participants.

Flipchart markers.

Procedure

TELL participants to follow these guidelines:

Individually, read the list of figures of speech.

As a group, decide what is being described by each figure of speech.

Decide through discussion on a positive, work-related outcome or pattern of behavior you wish to describe.

Develop a figure of speech to describe it.

CALL TIME after about 12 minutes.

Debrief

REVIEW the table group discussion by:

- Call out the number of each item on the list. Call on one table group to identify the feeling or behavior pattern described. Call on the other groups to agree, disagree, modify, amplify.

- When the review is complete call on each table group to share their figures of speech.

- After each is read aloud ask the rest of the group to identify what this figure of speech brings to mind. Then have the "owner" describe the action or behavior pattern they wanted to describe.

- When all groups have finished, ask participants to discuss the activity—how difficult was it, how effective the figures of speech were in creating mental images and conveying meaning.

  You're looking for: *images are hard to come up with without practice, are very economical, they involve the listener.*

Images Are Everywhere

Here is a list of commonly used figures of speech. What does each one describe?

It/he/she/ is:

1   slow as molasses

2   like lightening

3   thunderstruck

4   not even in the same ballpark

5   sleeping like a baby

6   looking for an escape hatch

7   shaking like a leaf

8   up to…neck in alligators

9   on cloud nine

10   turned to stone

11   on pins and needles

12   prickly as a porcupine.

Some event or object is/performs:

13   purrs like a kitten

14   like greased lightening

15   a port in a storm

16   helping hand

17   light at the end of the tunnel

18   etched in stone

19   as clear as mud

20   crystal clear.

As a group, describe an aspect of your responsibility, or someone's activity on the team in terms of a figure of speech. When complete, write it on a flipchart.

_____

_____

_____

_____

_____

Favorite Things Activity Guidelines

Objective(s)   This activity creates participant awareness of:

- Our perceptions and feelings, to which, in everyday life, we are often not tuned-in.

- A multitude of non-lead-like outcomes result from this lack of attention.

Time   10 minutes.

Materials   For this activity, nothing is needed beyond "A Few of My Favorite Things" on page 143.

Procedure

 TELL participants to follow these guidelines:

- Individually, quickly compile your lists

- If nothing comes to mind, go to the next list

- You've got five minutes, so write as fast as you can. Use shorthand, if you can.

 CALL TIME after 5 minutes.

Debrief *REVIEW* with the entire group by asking questions such as:

- Those who did not have five items in one of the lists, raise hands.

- Those who did not have five items in two, (three), (four), (five), (six) of the lists, raise hands.

- Which categories were most difficult—your likes or dislikes?

- Most likely, participants will have had a harder time with the positives than the negatives.

- Would anyone like to hazard a guess as to why these lists might be hard for us?

- The point you want them to reach here is that we don't pay attention to our own opinions and feelings.

- Where do you think this habit of not paying attention to ourselves comes from?

MAKE THE POINT that attending to our responses is *crucial* to having *insight* and *vision*.

A Few of My Favorite Things

As quickly as possible, off the top of your head, complete these lists. If nothing comes to mind just move to the next list. Use short-hand, or simple notes to remind yourself what you mean. No agonizing!

My five favorite pastimes are:

1 _____

2 _____

3 _____

4 _____

5 _____

My five favorite foods are:

1 _____

2 _____

3 _____

4 _____

5 _____

My five favorite things about work are:

1 _____

2 _____

3 _____

4 _____

5 _____

My five *least* favorite things about work are:

1 _____

2 _____

3 _____

4 _____

5 _____

My five favorite things about where I live are:

1 _____

2 _____

3 _____

4 _____

5 _____

My five *least* favorite things about where I live are:

1 _____

2 _____

3 _____

4 _____

5 _____

Notes after the discussion:

_____

_____

_____

_____

_____

Values Activity Guidelines

Objective(s)

This activity provides participants with an opportunity to identify:

- What they value most
- How their values guide their decisions
- How those values differ from those of others.

Time

30 minutes.

Materials

For this activity participants need "It's Up to Us to Decide" on page 146, and each *group* needs a blank flipchart.

Procedure

TELL participants to join a table group.

ASSIGN a case to each table group.

PROVIDE these guidelines:

- Individually, read the case assigned to your table group.
- When finished, rank the described "offenses" from *least* to *most* acceptable.
- As a group, discuss your perceptions and reach a consensus on the most acceptable item(s).

RECORD your responses on a flipchart, keeping your flipchart out of view.

CALL TIME after about 20 minutes.

Debrief

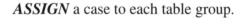

REVIEW the table group discussion by:

Call on a spokesperson for each group to report on their case, the conclusions they reached, and why.

ASK participants to comment on:

- Ease or difficulty they had in reaching consensus.
- Amount of variability in their group.
- How strongly they felt about the values that were the underpinning for their decisions.
- Were they aware of their attachment to these values prior to the activity.

CONCLUDE by asking participants to list their own values as they become aware of them in this activity.

It's Up to Us to Decide

Read the case assigned to your group. Identify the behaviors in your case that you believe inappropriate. Rank them in order from least to most acceptable. Then discuss the issues with your group. Try to come to a consensus about the list. The important thing in this discussion is to identify why (the underlying value) each issue ranks as it does with you.

Case One

Mary Melody is *vice president of sales* for a small software company, BridgeWare. BridgeWare sells its products through national shows, aimed at its industry (banking) and via telephone sales efforts. BridgeWare has an excellent reputation and updates its products annually to accommodate new IRS and other rulings. In addition, BridgeWare does major revisions of the existing software and introduces new products on an ongoing basis.

Mary has organized her sales force into two sales groups, *new account* and *reorder*. As a result, more than one representative may be calling an existing customer, one to upgrade existing products and the other to sell new products. BridgeWare subscribes to the *lifetime value of a customer* theory and look at satisfying their existing customers as crucial to their ongoing success. New sales are equally important, as they hold the key to current and future growth. New account sales representatives have a richer compensation package than the *reorder* sales group.

Recently several issues have come to light which have upset Mary and her boss, Wayne Bridge. Among these are:

- Two new account sales representatives have been found to have falsified exhibit sales contact numbers.

- The same representatives have also been found to have submitted falsified expense reports.

- A third representative (from the same group) appears to be carrying on an affair with a show acquaintance. Telephone logs indicate that there are frequent and lengthy daily calls from BridgeWare's offices to this individual.

- At the same time *reorder* sales people have been found to be crossing the line from upgrade sales to selling additional, new, software to existing clients. They have been getting the commissions that go with these sales. *New accounts* representatives are angry with them.

- At the same time, a competitor has called, accusing one of Mary's sales reps of spying. When questioned, the representative has admitted to doing so, and freely acknowledges doing this on his own initiative. The competitor is threatening to sue.

- Meanwhile, Mary herself has submitted an unjustifiably rosy forecast, because she knows that this will influence the budgeting cycle currently under way. By over-forecasting, Mary hopes to receive budgeting for several items next year that she otherwise wouldn't have.

Case Two

Janie has taught school for ten years. Each year is the same. Only the problems change, though they remain irritatingly familiar. At this stage, Janie is *bored* with the job. But it offers good hours and excellent benefits—things she does not want to lose. It affords her time for hobbies—photography, theater, and physical conditioning. It is secure, and allows her to buy many of the things she likes. However, there are days when she wonders if the lack of stimulation the job provides is worth the security it affords.

From Janie's perspective, the problem is that it now takes real discipline to keep class records, prepare for class, be on time, be enthusiastic—to keep motivated. She knows she's no star teacher, but it's not as if she is trying to be nominated *teacher of the year*. She suspects that her students are just as bored as she is, but she's given up trying to supply *their* motivation. As far as she's concerned, they either have it or they don't!

She and another teacher have come up with a plan that may diminish the workload even further. They have similar assignments. They will jointly prepare for class, and share materials. This should cut preparation time in half.

Janie also has hit upon a plan to delegate paperwork to some of her better students—she will have one keep attendance records, and has made arrangements to have another score papers and enter grades in her grade book four days a week. That way she can forget about it until it's time to submit the records to her supervisor. Now, all that's left is making it to the classroom on time. She hasn't quite figured out a way to get around that one. In fact, she's been "dinged" once this semester for being late, so she's going to have to watch it.

Inappropriate behaviors

_____

_____

_____

_____

_____

_____

_____

_____

_____

My Values

Based on the previous activity, choose five values from the list that are important to you. Note how they influence you.

achievement _____

altruism _____

autonomy _____

courage _____

courtesy _____

dependability _____

family _____

fidelity _____

freedom _____

harmony _____

health _____

honesty _____

integrity _____

justice _____

knowledge _____

kindness _____

love _____

loyalty _____

morality _____

physical appearance _____

pleasure _____

originality _____

respect _____

security _____

self-discipline _____

self-reliance _____

skill _____

unselfishness _____

wealth _____

Vision Activity Guidelines

Objective(s)   This activity provides participants with an opportunity to identify:

- How visions grow.
- How effective visions are communicated.

Time   20 minutes.

Materials   For this activity no additional supplies are needed beyond "Case One" on the next page.

Procedure   *TELL* participants to work in table groups, following these guidelines:

- Individually, read the two cases.
- As a group, choose to work on either *Case One* or *Case Two*.
- As a group, decide if what is being described represents a vision. Support your conclusion.

CALL TIME after about 12 minutes.

Debrief

REVIEW the table group discussion by:

- Call on a spokesperson for each group to report on the case they worked on, the conclusions they reached, and their judgment about:

  - The presence or absence of vision, and
  - The effectiveness of how it's been communicated.

LIST participant responses on a flipchart under the headings "qualities of a vision" and "communicated effectively."

Possible Uses   If you decide to use this activity as a stand-alone piece, you should precede it with these two handouts:

- "How Vision Develops" on page 121.
- "How to Communicate the Vision" on page 123.

Which One Is a Vision

Read each of the following cases. Decide how it represents a vision in action.

Case One

John Stamp is a retired college professor who has opened a glass and screen shop in a building he has owned for many years. It is on the edge of a seedy neighborhood that was affluent before easy transportation and affordable houses in the suburbs drew people away. John has always enjoyed puttering, and has dramatically improved the place since he opened shop. He says he finally has an honest job.

Now that everything has been fixed, there are days when he is not busy, when he has nothing to do but listen to the radio. Thus his new passion. On his local public radio station he was listening to an interview with an author who studied and wrote about the lives of inner city children and how society neglects them. John was moved by the author's compassion, and could relate to what he was talking about from his knowledge of children in his business neighborhood.

Over the next several weeks, through conversations with customers and neighborhood business people, John found himself fixing up an empty space in his building for an after-school supervised homework program for latch-key children. His cohorts in this endeavor are retired people like himself, who see an opportunity to make a statement about what's been happening to education in this country while helping to lower the crime rate. They call themselves "The Grannies," which they are.

They installed armchairs for themselves, and school desks that they bought at a swap meet. Some of the grandmothers expect to make cookies, and a local market has volunteered milk and fruit for afternoon snacks. The grandparents are starting small—with just eight second and third graders.

They sit and chat each afternoon before their charges arrive. When the children come, each has a "grandparent" to talk to about school, to listen to them read, ask them to spell, and sometimes even read stories to them.

John is so excited about what is happening that he's asked to talk to the city council about publicizing his idea. He now believes the "grannie" program should be expanded throughout the neighborhood.

What aspects of leadership and vision does John demonstrate?

Case Two

Stephen Rowan is a swimming instructor at a local youth club. He teaches 10- to 12-year olds and coaches a water polo team. While barely more than a teenager himself, his students look up to him.

Stephen is very serious about physical fitness. He believes that people are polluting their bodies with cigarettes and junk food. He never misses an opportunity to reinforce these ideas. At every lesson, he asks his students what they had for lunch and is quick to suggest alternatives they might like. He tells them how these more wholesome foods will enhance their endurance. Likewise he constantly warns against smoking.

Because his charges look up to Stephen, they have started to reject hot dogs and similar former favorites. Some have started asking their moms for more fruit and question what she plans to serve for meals. Since many of the parents hold full time jobs in addition to their parenting role, they don't appreciate the "help." Parents whose smoking habits have become targets of their children's crusade to reform them are even more irritated. They have begun to receive lectures about the evils of smoking. They have "had enough!"

As a result, many have complained to the recreation director. They have cited Stephen's "values based" mission as irrelevant and meddlesome. They threaten to pull their children out of the water if Stephen doesn't change his ways.

What aspects of leadership and leadership vision does Stephen exemplify? How effectively has he shared the vision?

_____

_____

_____

_____

_____

_____

_____

_____

_____

Preferences Activity Guidelines

Objective(s)   This role play provides participants an opportunity to practice:

- Focusing on individual team member's strengths and preferences.
- Using effective communication skills to gather information.

Time   30 minutes.

Materials   For this activity no additional supplies are needed beyond the activity "Finding Out People's Preferences" on page 153.

Procedure   *TELL* participants they will work in pairs to conduct this role play.

ASK participants to count off in twos. A *one* and a *two* constitute a working pair.

- Individually, read the directions.
- *Ones* start the interview. As you listen, take notes. If something is unclear, ask for:

  Clarification: *What do you mean by that? Could you say more about that?*

  An example: *Could you give me an example?*

- *Twos* answer the questions truthfully.
- You have 10 minutes for each round.

 CALL TIME after 10 and 20 minutes.

Debrief

REVIEW the role play experience by asking questions such as:

- How did you feel about being asked about your strengths—what you enjoy, what you are good at, what you learn easily?
- Do you do this at work? Why, or why not?
- What implication does this have for *role* and *responsibility?*

Finding Out People's Preferences

Some people are not used to thinking about their strengths—they often depend on others to tell them. To help such a person become aware may require approaching the topic from different angles. Start by exploring the most obvious topic, and then, from a cause-effect perspective, explore some of the effects of a talent or strength. The following sequence may help you develop your line of thinking:

1   Principle strength or talent

2   Activities most enjoyed

3   Activities you are best at

4   Things learned most easily (facile learning is an indicator of talent)

5   Activities which cause time to stand still or to fly

6   Dreaded, disliked, most difficult, and avoided activities.

Questions You Wish to Ask

_____

_____

_____

_____

_____

_____

Notes About Yourself

_____

_____

_____

_____

_____

_____

Visualization Activity Guidelines

Objective(s)   This activity provides participants an opportunity to practice:

- Visualizing a future event.
- Developing images of a future possibility.

Time   20 minutes: 15 minutes guided visualization and note taking, 5 minutes debriefing.

Materials   *All* the participants need for this activity is something they care about, blank paper, and a writing instrument.

Procedure   *TELL* participants to close their eyes. Slowly read this to them:

- You are going to do something about this issue that's been hanging.
- What are you going to do about it (pause)?
- Who are you talking to about it (pause)? What are you saying (pause)? What are they saying (pause)? How are you undertaking your project (pause)?
- *Fast-forward:*
  - It is six months from now. You've taken action. People are giving you credit for what you have done.
  - Who are these people?
  - Where are you gathered?
  - Who is that getting up to recognize you?
  - Can you hear what he or she is saying (pause)?
  - The voice is describing what you did (pause).
  - How you persevered (pause).
  - Someone is taking your picture (pause). What are you wearing? How do you look in that picture?
  - Someone asks you to tell everyone how you did it(pause).
  - You're standing up. You're beginning to tell about the experience (pause).
  - You're thanking people who were involved, who supported you (pause). Who are they?
  - How do you feel (pause)?
  - How do others feel about you (pause)?
  - Now open your eyes.

ASK participants to individually:

- Describe what they accomplished
- What images they saw
- Their feelings
- How others responded to them.

Debrief

 REVIEW the activity by asking questions such as:

- What did you visualize?

  Accept a few volunteers.

- Are you more likely to act on this issue now? Why or why not?

  Anticipate a few people saying that they will now do something about it because of the positive image of the outcome they visualized.

- When you have visualized taking actions like this in the past, have your visualizations been *positive* or *negative*?

  Anticipate negative.

- How does that affect you?

  Negative visualizations discourage action.

Risk Taking Activity Guidelines

Objective(s)   This activity causes participants to:

- Face a risk that intimidates them.

- Work on self-encouragement.

Time   20 minutes.

Materials   For this activity you need colored markers at each table as well as copies of "I Think I Can" on page 157.

Procedure   *TELL* participants that for this activity they will work in table groups.

ASK participants if they remember the little train that could. Have someone tell the story.

TELL participants that each table is going to construct such a train, powered by their united courage. Each member of the group adds one carriage to the train.

- Individually, identify the *freight* you are loading onto your carriage. This is a *risk* you would like to take, but have been afraid to.

- Place warning signs ("Highly Volatile!") or other decorations on your railcar. Color it as time allows.

- As a table, decide what to name your train—e.g., Reliability Railway, Freedom Express, Courtesy Coaster, etc.

- Post your train close to your table. Hitch your wagons to the engine. Then we'll talk about it.

 CALL TIME after 8 and 10 minutes.

Debrief   *REVIEW* the activity by having each table tell the others about their railway and how the "I think I can" engine is going to pull their risk-taking freight.

I Think I Can

Freight Manifest

Signaling Activity Guidelines

Objective(s)	This activity provides participants with the realization that:
- Everything you do or don't do broadcasts subtext about yourself.
- People read that information, whether or not we intend it.

Time

10 minutes.

Materials

Prior to the session, cut up a class list so that each participant's name appears on a single folded piece of paper. Place these names in a container. If you want to, place your own name in the container. This will mean that you will also draw a name.

Procedure

TELL participants to write the name they drew from the container at the top of the activity sheet "You're Signaling" on page 159.

ASK participants to answer the questions with the first thing that pops into their minds, to not filter it too much.

 CALL TIME after 5 minutes.

COLLECT the papers.

DISTRIBUTE the pages by calling out the names on the top.

GIVE participants a moment to read what was written.

Debrief

ASK participants to comment on:

- Did you have to think about what to write?
- Were you aware that you were gathering and processing so much information about others?
- Were you surprised by what you read about yourself?
- Do any of you feel that you don't want to send some of the signals that another received from you?
  - If so, what will you do differently in the future?

You're Signaling

Name: _____

Complete the following for the person whose name you wrote on the line above.

1 Your *style of dress* suggests to me that you

_____

2 From your *grooming* I'd guess that you

_____

3 Your *posture* during the session seems to indicate that you

_____

4 They way you *talk* makes me think that you

_____

5 The way you *listen* tells me that you

_____

6 Your *gestures* give me the impression that you

_____

7 Your *promptness* (or lack of it) for the session suggests to me that you

_____

8 From your level of *eye contact* I'd guess that you

_____

9 From your level of *attention* I think that you probably

_____

10 From your level of *involvement*, I'd say that you

_____

11 From the way you *interact* with others in the session, I imagine that you

_____

Constructive Feedback Role Play Guidelines

Objective(s)

This activity provides opportunity for participants to practice:

- Giving corrective feedback in a positive, constructive manner.
- Experiencing what it feels like to receive constructive feedback.

Time

30 minutes—5 minutes preparation, 10 minutes for each round (7 for the role play and 3 for feedback) and 5 minutes to debrief.

Materials

You may wish to list the above times on a flipchart and display it at the beginning of the practice session.

Procedure

TELL participants they will work in pairs to conduct this practice activity.

ASK participants to count off in twos. A *one* and a *two* constitute a working pair. (Make sure people work with a different partner than they had for the past activity.)

- Individually, read the directions and prepare your statements and questions.
- *Twos* start the interview by briefing *ones* on the background of the situation you will use.
- *Ones,* you may improvise in responding to questions.
- Complete the feedback with an agreement.

CALL TIME for feedback at 7 minutes, and round two at 10 minutes.

Debrief

REVIEW the activity by asking questions such as:

- How did you feel about receiving feedback?
- How did it feel to give feedback?
- Is it appropriate for peers to exchange this type of feedback?

Giving Constructive Feedback

Think of a situation you are experiencing in your job (or personal life) where you want to take corrective action:

_____

_____

1　Make a direct statement indicating what the behavior/performance level is and why it is a problem.

_____

_____

_____

2　Write what you imagine the person would say is causing this behavior.

_____

_____

_____

3　Discuss (back and forth) the imagined consequences if the behavior/performance level continues.

_____

_____

_____

4　Write how you imagine the person would identify what he/she can do to change the behavior. Set levels and timeframes.

_____

_____

_____

5　Agree to follow-up action and review date.

_____

_____

_____

Crediting Role Play Guidelines

Objective(s)   This activity provides opportunity for participants to:

- Practice giving credit for small and significant accomplishments.

- Experience what it feels like to receive positive feedback.

Time   25 minutes—5 minutes preparation, 8 minutes for each round (6 for the role play and 2 for feedback), and 4 minutes to debrief.

Materials   You may wish to list the above times on a flipchart and display it at the beginning of the practice session. Provide participants a copy of "Giving Credit" on page 163.

Procedure   *TELL* participants they will work in pairs to conduct this practice activity.

ASK participants count off in twos. A *one* and a *two* constitute a working pair. (Make sure people work with a different partner than they had for the past activity.)

- Individually, read the directions and prepare your statements and questions.

- *Twos* start the interview by briefing *ones* on the background of situation.

 CALL TIME for feedback at 7 minutes and round two at 10 minutes.

Debrief   *REVIEW* the activity by asking questions such as:

- How did you feel about receiving positive feedback?

- How did it feel to give positive feedback?

- Is it appropriate for peers to exchange this type of feedback? To give it to those higher than you in the chain-of-command?

- Where else in your life might you use this skill?

Giving Credit

Think of a situation you are experiencing in your job (or personal life) where you want to give credit to someone:

_____

_____

1   **Step One:** Name the person and identify the accomplishment you wish to acknowledge.

_____

_____

_____

2   **Step Two:** Identify specific aspects of the person's behavior that led to this outcome.

_____

_____

3   **Step Three:** Identify why that behavior led to the result accomplished, and why that is important.

_____

_____

_____

4   **Step Four:** Summarize the value of what the person has done.

_____

_____

_____

Impact of Receiving Credit

Jot down how you felt when you were given credit.

_____

_____

Notes to Yourself

_____

_____

_____

_____

_____

_____

_____

_____

_____

_____

_____

_____

_____

Chapter Nine:

Instruments and Assessments

This *Leadership: ASTD Trainer's Sourcebook* chapter provides instruments and trainer notes you can use for a variety of assessments focused on various aspects of leadership. Use these as part of the training designs offered earlier in this book. Use them with other training materials, or as suggested in Chapter 1.

How to Use Instruments & Assessments

… including:

As part of one of the training designs provided in this book.

As pre-work, as a means of stimulating interest in upcoming training sessions.

As follow-up, to reinforce training already conducted.

As 360-degree feedback to participants, giving them insight into how others view them.

Chapter structure Each instrument in this chapter contains these elements:

- Objective
- Time required
- Materials you will need
- Procedure
- Alternatives (if appropriate).

Leadership Assessment Guidelines

Objective(s)   This instrument provides participants with insight and feedback on:

- What leadership characteristics they embody.

- Their leadership strengths and weaknesses.

Time   30 minutes.

Material   Participants need only the handout on the following page(s), and a pen or pencil.

Procedure   *TELL* participants to follow these guidelines:

- Read each descriptor and circle a representative number from the rating scale.

- When finished, follow the directions on "Rating Your Self-Assessment Scores" on page 169.

- When you have calculated your totals for each characteristic, connect your scores in a graph format.

    CALL TIME after about 8–10 minutes.

TELL participants to take a moment to consider what they might like to change in this picture.

Alternative   *As a 360-degree* instrument, *FILL IN* the individual's name on 4 to 6 copies of "Leadership Assessment (Other)" on page 167. Include an equal number of self-addressed envelopes, with a return date clearly marked on the envelope. Ask the participant to distribute these instruments to people in the workplace who know them well. When the instruments are returned, before the training session:

1   Calculate a score for each trait, by combining the rating for the appropriate questions from all respondents and dividing by the number of respondents.

2   Place the scores on "Rating Your Self-Assessment Scores" on page 169. Circle the appropriate numbers, and connect the circles with straight lines, to form a graph.

3   Have the participants graph their answers on rating sheets during the training session.

4   Discuss differences in perception.

Leadership Assessment (Other)

Name of person being rated: _____

To the best of your knowledge, rate the person on a scale of 1 to 5 for each item.

		Rarely		Sometimes		Always
1	He/she is curious about how others see/do things.	1	2	3	4	5
2	He/she can see common meaning in diverse opinions.	1	2	3	4	5
3	He/she encourages others to come to their own conclusions about things, supports them when they do so.	1	2	3	4	5
4	If he/she expects someone to behave in a certain way, he/she is willing to act in that way him/herself.	1	2	3	4	5
5	He/she gives people positive feedback when he/she notices their good actions.	1	2	3	4	5
6	He/she is open to lots of different opinions, not just own.	1	2	3	4	5
7	When he/she sees the importance of what he/she is doing, he/she shares it with others.	1	2	3	4	5
8	He/she tries to give people the help they need and want, so they can be more effective in what they are doing.	1	2	3	4	5
9	He/she leads by example, not just by words.	1	2	3	4	5
10	He/she makes sure we celebrate as a team when we meet milestones.	1	2	3	4	5
11	He/she encourages others to find new and interesting approaches to things.	1	2	3	4	5
12	When working on important things he/she enlists others' help, by stressing the importance of the task.	1	2	3	4	5
13	When people are getting things wrong, he/she takes the time to help them figure out what they need to change and how they can fix the problem.	1	2	3	4	5
14	He/she is persistent as a way to help others not lose heart.	1	2	3	4	5
15	He/she encourages team fun; we enjoy working together.	1	2	3	4	5

Leadership Assessment (Self)

Name of person being rated: _____

To the best of your knowledge, rate yourself on a scale of 1 to 5 for each item.

		Rarely	Sometimes		Always
1	I am curious about how others see things and why they do them.	1 2	3	4	5
2	I can usually see common threads of meaning in diverse opinions.	1 2	3	4	5
3	I encourage others to come to their own conclusions about things. I support them when they do.	1 2	3	4	5
4	If I expect someone to behave in a certain way I am willing to act in that way.	1 2	3	4	5
5	I give people positive feedback when I notice their good actions.	1 2	3	4	5
6	I am open to differing opinions, not just my own.	1 2	3	4	5
7	When I see the importance of what I am doing, I share that with others.	1 2	3	4	5
8	I try to give people the help they need and want, so that they can be more effective in what they are doing.	1 2	3	4	5
9	I lead by example, not just by words.	1 2	3	4	5
10	I make sure we celebrate as a team when we meet milestones.	1 2	3	4	5
11	I encourage others to find new and interesting approaches.	1 2	3	4	5
12	When working on important things, I enlist the help of others by sharing with them the importance of what we're doing.	1 2	3	4	5
13	When someone is getting things wrong, I take the time to help them figure out what they need to change and how they can fix the problem.	1 2	3	4	5
14	I persist in helping others to not to lose heart.	1 2	3	4	5
15	I try to encourage fun as a team, so that we all have a good time working together.	1 2	3	4	5

Rating Your Self-Assessment Scores

Sum the scores you gave yourself on questions identified in the second to last row of each column of the grid below. Enter each score in its appropriate column by circling the printed number. Complete for each column. Then draw straight lines to connect the circles. The resulting graph presents a picture of your own perception of your leadership profile across the five characteristics which we identify in these sessions.

15	15	15	15	15
14	14	14	14	14
13	13	13	13	13
12	12	12	12	12
11	11	11	11	11
10	10	10	10	10
9	9	9	9	9
8	8	8	8	8
7	7	7	7	7
6	6	6	6	6
5	5	5	5	5
4	4	4	4	4
3	3	3	3	3
2	2	2	2	2
1	1	1	1	1
Questions 1, 6, 11	**Questions 2, 7, 12**	**Questions 3, 8, 13**	**Questions 4, 9, 14**	**Questions 5, 10, 15**
Questions Groupthink	**Resets Direction**	**Guides Cooperative Action**	**Walks the Talk**	**Motivates Others**

When used as a 360-degree assessment, calculate the totals for each characteristic from the answers of the other respondents. Then divide by the number of respondents. Enter these totals and connect them in a chart, using a second color.

Notes to Yourself

Based on your self-scoring, which of the leadership characteristics would you like to improve? How might you do this?

_____

_____

_____

Paradigm Self-Assessment Guidelines

Objective(s)

This self-assessment provides participants an opportunity to assess:

- Their awareness level about the views they have learned in each category.

- How they accept or challenge these views.

Time

15 minutes.

Materials

Only the self-assessment is required.

Procedure

TELL participants to follow guidelines at the top of the self-assessment:

> If participants have questions, direct their attention to the example at the bottom of the page.

> Discuss until people are comfortable with the directions.

CALL TIME after about 12 minutes.

ASK participants to volunteer any insights this activity provides them.

Alternative use

This activity is not called out in any of the training designs. You may choose to use it with a group that you believe behaves in very stereotypical ways, or with people who have a low level of self-awareness, and are unaware of it.

Paradigm Self-Assessment

This self-assessment is designed to see how aware you are of the social scripts (paradigms) you hold about yourself and the world around you; for example, you might recognize that you have a traditionally stereotypical concept of what is appropriate behavior for males and for females. How aware are you of the degree to which your views on this subject are stereotypical? How much do you challenge your stereotypic views in your personal actions, in professional assignments and requests, and in the behavior of others? Are you aware of them and do you challenge any of them?

Rate yourself in each of the areas:

7 is *very aware or challenge vigorously.*

4 is *not sure.*

1 is *don't have any pre-conceptions in this area* or *have nothing to challenge.*

Paradigms	Awareness Level	Challenge Level
General		
Self-concept	1 2 3 4 5 6 7	1 2 3 4 5 6 7
Appearance	1 2 3 4 5 6 7	1 2 3 4 5 6 7
Character traits	1 2 3 4 5 6 7	1 2 3 4 5 6 7
Social skills	1 2 3 4 5 6 7	1 2 3 4 5 6 7
Intellectual capability	1 2 3 4 5 6 7	1 2 3 4 5 6 7
Success potential	1 2 3 4 5 6 7	1 2 3 4 5 6 7
Professional Self-Concept		
Interpersonal skills	1 2 3 4 5 6 7	1 2 3 4 5 6 7
Technical skills	1 2 3 4 5 6 7	1 2 3 4 5 6 7
Work ethic	1 2 3 4 5 6 7	1 2 3 4 5 6 7
Growth potential	1 2 3 4 5 6 7	1 2 3 4 5 6 7
Popularity	1 2 3 4 5 6 7	1 2 3 4 5 6 7
Social Paradigms Ethnicity	1 2 3 4 5 6 7	1 2 3 4 5 6 7
Sexually appropriate roles	1 2 3 4 5 6 7	1 2 3 4 5 6 7
Age related roles	1 2 3 4 5 6 7	1 2 3 4 5 6 7
Authority level roles	1 2 3 4 5 6 7	1 2 3 4 5 6 7

Listening Assessment Guidelines

Objective(s)

This assessment creates participant awareness of:

- Their typical behavior on the various dimensions of listening.
- Areas where they can improve their listening skills.

Time

10 minutes.

Materials

Nothing is needed beyond "Listening Self-Assessment" on page 173 (if being used as a self-assessment.)

If being used as a 360-degree assessment, be sure to be available to participants to coach them on the results they receive, and:

1 Send 4 to 6 copies of the "Listening Skills Assessment—Other" to the participant with self-addressed stamped envelopes that are clearly labeled with a *return-by* date.

2 Enter the participant's name at the top of each assessment.

3 Include a note to the participant instructing him/her to give these assessments to people he/she knows well, asking them to provide him/her with honest feedback.

4 Complete a rating page for the participant, using an average of scores for each question.

Procedure

TELL participants to follow these guidelines for the self-assessment version:

- Individually, provide a rating for each question.
- Be as honest and open-minded as possible.
- When complete, enter scores for the traits on "Listening Scores" on page 175.

CALL TIME after 8 minutes, or when most participants finish.

BE AVAILABLE to participants when they receive the feedback from the two assessments—self and other. People are often upset if self-perceptions differ radically from the way others see them. Point out that:

- The feedback is an opportunity for personal growth.
- Everyone can benefit from improved listening skills.

Alternatives

This assessment can be used in conjunction with any training design that emphasizes listening skills. It can be used as a self-assessment or in 360 format.

Listening Self-Assessment

To the best of your knowledge, rate yourself on a scale of 1 to 5 for each item.

		Rarely	Sometimes		Always	
1	I am available when people want to talk to me.	1	2	3	4	5
2	I am interested in what others have to say.	1	2	3	4	5
3	I pay close attention to what others say to me.	1	2	3	4	5
4	I ask people to contribute their opinions and to say what they really think and feel.	1	2	3	4	5
5	When people are talking I let them finish while listening attentively.	1	2	3	4	5
6	I gather input before making up my mind.	1	2	3	4	5
7	When I disagree with someone, I always value his/her opinions.	1	2	3	4	5
8	When others talk to me I fully understand what they are saying.	1	2	3	4	5
9	In conversation, I listen more than I talk.	1	2	3	4	5

Listening Assessment (Other)

Name of person being rated: _____

To the best of your knowledge, rate the person on a scale of 1 to 5 for each item.

		Rarely		Sometimes		Always
1	He/she is available when people want to talk to him/her.	1	2	3	4	5
2	He/she is interested in what I and others have to say.	1	2	3	4	5
3	He/she pays close attention to what I tell him/her.	1	2	3	4	5
4	He/she asks me and others to contribute our opinions and to say what we really think and feel.	1	2	3	4	5
5	When I'm talking to him/her, she/he lets me finish without interruption.	1	2	3	4	5
6	He/she gathers input from many people before making up his /her mind.	1	2	3	4	5
7	When he/she disagrees with me or others, he/she still values our opinions.	1	2	3	4	5
8	When I and others talk to him/her, he/she fully understands what we are saying.	1	2	3	4	5
9	In conversation, he/she listens more than he/she talks.	1	2	3	4	5

Listening Scores

*Name of person being rated:*_____

On the grid below, identify the score you gave yourself for each of the listening trait questions.

Question	Trait	Score				
1	Accessibility	1	2	3	4	5
2	Interest	1	2	3	4	5
3	Attentiveness	1	2	3	4	5
4	Encourages expression	1	2	3	4	5
5	Doesn't interrupt	1	2	3	4	5
6	Suspends judgment	1	2	3	4	5
7	Values differences	1	2	3	4	5
8	Shows empathy & understanding	1	2	3	4	5
9	Doesn't talk too much	1	2	3	4	5

Charting 360-degree feedback

If your name and a graph are already on this sheet, this represents the average for each question provided by all those who answered the questionnaire about you. (Total for each question divided by the number of respondents.) Enter your self-assessment results in another color and connect the numbers. The difference between the two graphs represents the difference between how you see yourself and how others see you.

Notes to yourself

Based on your self-scoring, which of your listening characteristics would you like to improve? How might you do it?

_____

_____

_____

_____

_____

Coaching Assessment Guidelines

Objective(s)

This activity provides participants an opportunity to practice:

- Determining a person's skill level, experience, and motivation in three job areas.

- Effective communication skills to gather information.

Time

20 minutes, 4 minutes individual preparation, and 8 minutes for each conversation.

Materials

No additional supplies are needed beyond "Coaching Assessment Questionnaire" on page 177.

Procedure

TELL participants they will work in pairs to conduct this practice activity.

ASK participants to count off in twos. A *one* and a *two* constitute a working pair. Make sure people work with a different partner than in the last activity.

- Individually, read the directions and answer the preparatory questions.

- *Twos* start the interview by inviting *ones* to talk about areas of responsibility. They may not use labels (*high*, *medium,* or *low*) As you listen, take notes. If something is unclear, ask for:

    Clarification: *What do you mean by that? Would you say more about that?*

    An example: *Would you give me an example?*

- Answer questions truthfully.

- Switch roles after 8 minutes.

 CALL TIME at 8 and 16 minutes.

Debrief

REVIEW the activity by asking questions such as:

- Did you and the person you were working with have the same level of skill, experience, and motivation for each aspect of the job you talked about? What implication does this have for your coaching?[1]

---

1   For more see *Coaching: The ASTD Trainer's Sourcebook* by Dennis C. Kinlaw.

Coaching Assessment Questionnaire

Relative to their positions, everybody has varying degrees of capability for each of their assigned responsibilities. A salesperson may be excellent in face-to-face selling, but close to incompetent in writing letters and proposals. A manager might be strong in planning and scheduling, but uncomfortable giving feedback. The leader-coach must determine where to focus his/her efforts, and what type of coaching to provide.

List three different activities required of you in your job. For each, check the level of your *skill, experience,* and *motivation.*

Responsibility _____

Your level of	High	Med	Low
Skill			
Experience			
Motivation			

Responsibility _____

Your level of	High	Med	Low
Skill			
Experience			
Motivation			

Responsibility _____

Your level of	High	Med	Low
Skill			
Experience			
Motivation			

Interview Guide

Ask your partners to identify three different areas of their jobs and to, in general terms, describe how they feel about their competence, experience, and motivation without labeling it (*high, medium*, or *low*). Ask questions to clarify when you wish. When complete, your grids should mirror how the person you interviewed had marked him or herself.

Responsibility _____

Your level of	High	Med	Low
Skill			
Experience			
Motivation			

Responsibility _____

Your level of	High	Med	Low
Skill			
Experience			
Motivation			

Responsibility _____

Your level of	High	Med	Low
Skill			
Experience			
Motivation			

Notes _____

_____

_____

Goal Setting Self-Assessment Guidelines

Objective(s)   This activity provides participants an opportunity to:

- Identify leadership practices they need to improve.

- Behaviors they need to practice.

Time   15 minutes.

Materials   For this activity participants need "Leadership Characteristics" on page 180, feedback from their Leadership Practices assessment, and leadership training workshop experience.

Procedure   *TELL* participants to work individually.

REFER participants to the "Leadership Characteristics" on page 180.

PROVIDE these guidelines:

- Individually, identify your priority development areas.

- Behavior you need to practice if you are to develop that leadership characteristic.

- Under what circumstances, and how often you need practice it.

CALL TIME after about 12 minutes.

Debrief   *REVIEW* the self-assessment by inviting volunteers to:

Recognizing the characteristic they intend to develop.

Identifying behavior they need to practice.

Describing the circumstances and frequency of that practice.

Alternative use   This self-assessment planning tool can be used in many different training and development situations.

Leadership Characteristics

Here are the leadership characteristics we have reviewed in this session.

Question Groupthink by
- Being curious—investigating, asking *why*, asking questions, listening, verifying understanding, reflecting, and
- Taking initiative, risks, experimenting
- Being open to diverse opinions
- Encouraging creativity, innovation

Reset Direction by
- Developing a vision—synthesizing recurring themes and values, and
- *Selling* the vision—presenting a compelling vision of a possible future
- Enlisting others—asking for help, showing how they can make a difference

Guide Cooperative Action by
- Planning, setting team goals, and
- Empowering followers
- Encouraging initiative
- Delegating authority
- Coaching, monitoring
- Providing constructive feedback

Walk the Talk by
- Involvement—setting an example of personal commitment and
- Committing to quality outcomes
- Helping solve problems
- Being persistent

Motivate Ohers by
- Recognizing individual and team contributions
- Giving positive feedback
- Celebrating accomplishments
- Reinforcing teamwork

Which are your priority development areas?

1 _____

2 _____

3 _____

For each development area, identify

1 Area: _____

2 The behavior you intend to practice:

   _____

3 The circumstances and frequency you are aiming for:

   _____

   _____

1 Area: _____

2 The behavior you intend to practice:

   _____

3 The circumstances and frequency you are aiming for:

   _____

   _____

1 Area: _____

2 The behavior you intend to practice:

   _____

3 The circumstances and frequency you are aiming for:

   _____

   _____

Information Gathering Mode Assessment Guidelines

Objective(s)   This activity provides participants an opportunity to identify:

- How they gather information.

- Areas of information gathering that they might ignore.

Time   30 minutes.

Materials   For this activity no additional supplies are needed beyond "Information Gathering (Self)" on page 183 and 184.

Procedure   *TELL* participants to work to complete the self-assessment, following these guidelines:

Read each statement.

Indicate on the rating scale of 1–5 how true this statement is of you.

Do not over analyze any of the statements.

CALL TIME after about 12 minutes.

DIRECT participants to complete the analysis chart, using framework on the "Rating Your Scores" on page 184.

Debrief   *LEAD* a brief large group discussion by:

Call on volunteers to recall what they learned about themselves from this activity.

Alternative uses   You may use this as a stand-alone piece in coaching situations.

Information Gathering (Self)

Rate yourself for each item, to the best of your knowledge, using a scale from 1 to 5.

		Rarely		Sometimes		Always
1	I really understand something when I can get involved with doing it.	1	2	3	4	5
2	I need time to think about things, to sort out meanings.	1	2	3	4	5
3	When people tell me about their experiences, I understand what is going on.	1	2	3	4	5
4	Show me what you are explaining and I'll understand what you are saying.	1	2	3	4	5
5	I find reading about a problem—in a memo, article, or book—the best way to understand it.	1	2	3	4	5
6	To learn a new skill I usually have to play a role or simulation.	1	2	3	4	5
7	Sometimes the best way for me to understand a situation is to try to document it.	1	2	3	4	5
8	Once someone explains something, I understand it.	1	2	3	4	5
9	A videotape of a situation is a great way for me to absorb its full impact.	1	2	3	4	5
10	I usually ask people to put it in writing. That clarifies their thinking and I focus closer on the situation.	1	2	3	4	5
11	I usually ask people to let me experience what they are talking about.	1	2	3	4	5
12	I usually ask people to give me time to think about a situation they have described, so that I can decide what I think.	1	2	3	4	5
13	I usually ask people to tell me lots of details. That way I get a full picture of the situation.	1	2	3	4	5
14	I prefer people to show me what they are talking about.	1	2	3	4	5
15	I like to read a case study or article, because then I can grasp the information right away.	1	2	3	4	5

Rating Your Scores

Sum the scores you gave yourself on questions identified in the second to last row of each column of the grid below. Enter each score in its appropriate column by circling the printed number. Complete for each column. Then draw straight lines to connect the circles. The resulting graph presents a picture of your preferences for gathering information. The results are neither good nor bad, just something you should consider.

15	15	15	15	15
14	14	14	14	14
13	13	13	13	13
12	12	12	12	12
11	11	11	11	11
10	10	10	10	10
9	9	9	9	9
8	8	8	8	8
7	7	7	7	7
6	6	6	6	6
5	5	5	5	5
4	4	4	4	4
3	3	3	3	3
2	2	2	2	2
1	1	1	1	1
Questions 1, 6, 11	**Questions 2, 7, 12**	**Questions 3, 8, 13**	**Questions 4, 9, 14**	**Questions 5, 10, 15**
Doing; (Concrete Experience)	**Reflection**	**Listening to Others**	**Seeing Results**	**Reading**

Notes to Yourself

Based on your self-scoring, how can you compensate for information gathering techniques you do not use? How might you answer that you get information in ways that are most easy for you to grasp?

_____

_____

_____

_____

Opportunities to Celebrate Assessment Guidelines

Objective(s)

This assessment provides participants opportunity to identify how well they:

- Note completion of team goals and milestones.
- Celebrate team accomplishments.

Time

15 minutes.

Materials

Only the assessment, "Opportunities to Celebrate Successes" on page 186, and "Rating Your Scores" on page 187 are needed.

Procedure

TELL participants to read the questions and answer them as honestly as they can.

CALL TIME after 10 minutes.

Debrief

CALL on volunteers to discuss:

What did they find out about how well you celebrate successes?

What difference does celebration of success make?

Opportunities to Celebrate Successes

Rate yourself for each item, to the best of your knowledge, on a scale of 1 to 5.

		Rarely	Sometimes		Always
1	Projects are well planned and interim checkpoints/milestones are identified.	1	2	3 4	5
2	Milestones are put on the calendar and made a major review point.	1	2	3 4	5
3	When team members meet milestone schedules, we make that known to everyone.	1	2	3 4	5
4	Milestones are recognized with some type of celebration.	1	2	3 4	5
5	We circulate birthday cards, have birthday cakes, and other celebration for birthdays of team members.	1	2	3 4	5
6	We post calendars on which we mark the dates of all deadlines.	1	2	3 4	5
7	Everyone knows when deadlines occur.	1	2	3 4	5
8	We note *phase completions* on posted calendars.	1	2	3 4	5
9	We give people some type of emblem to celebrate meeting deadlines.	1	2	3 4	5
10	We mark anniversaries and other special dates with some type of celebration.	1	2	3 4	5

Rating Your Scores

Sum the scores you gave yourself on questions identified in the second to last row of each column of the grid below. Enter each score in its appropriate column by circling the printed number. Complete for each column. Then draw straight lines to connect the circles. The resulting graph presents a picture of your strengths and weaknesses in celebrating team successes.

10	10	10	10	10
9	9	9	9	9
8	8	8	8	8
7	7	7	7	7
6	6	6	6	6
5	5	5	5	5
4	4	4	4	4
3	3	3	3	3
2	2	2	2	2
1	1	1	1	1
Questions 1, 6	**Questions 2, 7**	**Questions 3, 8**	**Questions 4, 9**	**Questions 5, 10**
Identify Milestones	**Monitor Milestones**	**Announce Milestone Completions**	**Celebrate Interim Steps**	**Celebrate Personal Occasions**

Notes to Yourself

Based on your self-scoring, how can you improve your celebration of team success? What is your weakest link?

_____

_____

_____

_____

Chapter Ten:
Overhead Transparencies

This *Leadership: ASTD Trainer's Sourcebook* chapter contains overhead transparency masters referred to in Chapters 4, 5, and 6. These overheads serve to reinforce key concepts being discussed in the workshop designs. You can use them in follow-up designs of your own, or you may modify or add to them as needed. They include key content points taught in the learning designs presented here.

Use these Overheads

… by photocopying the pages onto transparencies. These are a minimum number of overheads. Add to them as you see fit. Use them in any of these ways:

Reproduced on paper, as handouts to participants, to be used for note taking.

As overhead transparencies, used to reinforce key concepts during the workshop sessions.

As overheads, to review concepts at the end of the training session, or at a later time.

One-Day Leadership Workshop

- Characteristics of leaders

- Based on your experiences/assignments

- Requiring your active participation

A Half-Day Leadership Workshop

Focus on *VISION*

- How we **develop** visions
- **Communicate** and
- **Reinforce** them

A One-Hour Leadership Workshop

Focus on *positive* reinforcement

Requiring your *active* participation

192

Leadership Characteristics

1 Question Groupthink

2 Reset Direction

3 Guide Cooperative Action

4 Walk the Talk

5 Motivate Others

Giving *Positive* Feedback

1 *Identify the result achieved*

2 *Describe specific examples*

3 *Identify why that is important*

4 *Express appreciation*

Agenda and Logistics

This workshop requires your

- *Full attention*
- *Active participation*
- *Consideration of others*
- *Prompt return from breaks or lunch*

Vision Defined

- **Vivid** image
- **Ideal** excellence
- **Future** orientation

Communicate the Vision

- **Prepare** a *vivid statement*—with images, key phrases, examples

- **Communicate** *enthusiastically* and often

- **Reinforce** frequently

Build on *Stren ths*

- *Match* roles to talents

- *Tailor* roles to team needs

- *Coach* to individual needs

Autonomy and Control

- *Determine where **control** is needed*

- *Identify where **initiative** is expected*

- *Encourage **autonomy** where possible*

199

Motivate the Team

- Build on *intrinsic* motivation
- Give *credit*
- Celebrate *milestones*
- Build *camaraderie*

Appendix

Resources for Training Professionals

Books

Batten, Joy D. *Tough-Minded Leadership*. New York: American Management Association, 1989.

Bennis, Warren, and Nanus, Burt. *Leaders*. New York: Harper & Row, 1985.

> Bennis has been at the forefront of the movement toward leadership. He's got numerous books and articles on the topic.

Bennis, Warren. *On Becoming a Leader*. New York: Addison-Wesley, 1989.

> As the title implies, this focuses on the forces that shape leaders.

Blanchard, Kenneth H., and Johnson, Spencer. *The One-Minute Manager*. New York: William Morrow &Company, Inc. 1982.

> Mangement techniques oriented, but complete and fast!

Cohen, William A. *The Art of the Leader*. New Jersey: Prentice Hall, 1990.

Covey, Stephen. *The Seven Habits of Highly Effective Leaders*. New York: Simon ans Schuster, 1989.

> You'll find a variety of audio-tapes from Covey available.

Crosby, Philip B. *Leading: The Art of Becoming an Executive*. New York: McGraw-Hill, 1990.

———. *Running Things: The Art of Making Things Happen*. New York: McGraw-Hill Book Company, 1986.

> Crosby is best known for his work on quality.

Gardner, John. *On Leaders*. New York: The Free Press, 1990.

Garfield, Charles. *Peak Performers: The New Heroes of American Business*. New York: William Morrow & Co., Inc., 1986.

Handy, Charles. *The Gods of Management*. London: Arrow Books Limited, 1995.

> Handy uses Greek gods to symbolize different styles of leadership and corporate culture. The book was first published in 1975 and has been republished four times. For many it is a "classic."

Hirsh, Sandra Krebs, and Kummerow, Jean M. *Introduction to Type in Organizations*, 2nd edition, Palo Alto: Consulting Psychologist Press, Inc., 1990

> For those who want to know more about personality types and how they affect our interactions in groups, this monograph is succinct and complete.

Hersey, Dr. Paul. *The Situational Leader: The Other 59 Minutes.* New York: Warner Books, 1984.

Hertzberg, Frederick. "Hertzberg on Motivation in the 1980s." *Industry Week* (October 1, 1979), pp.59-63.

———. *Work and the Nature of Man.* Cleveland: World, 1966.

Horton, Thomas R., and Peter C. Reid. *Beyond the Trust Gap.* Illinois: Business One Irwin, 1991.

Kotter, John P. *A Force for Change: How Leadership Differs from Management. New York:* The Free Press, 1990

———. *The Leadership Factor.* New York: Free Press, 1988.

> Kotter provides numerous and varied case examples.

Kouzes, James M., and Posner, Barry Z. *The Leadership Challenge.* San Francisco: Jossey-Bass Publishers, 1987.

> Kouzes and Posner do an excellent job of brining the leadership practices to life with numerous annecdotes and cases.

Kouzes, James M., Posner, Barry Z. *Credibility.* San Francisco: Jossey-Bass Publishers, 1995.

> For those who prefer to listen, you can find Kouzes' tape on this subject.

Peters, Tom. *Thriving on Chaos: A Handbook for a Management Revolution.* New York: Harper & Row, 1987.

Renesh, John. Ed. *New Traditions in Business: Spirit and Leadership in the 21st Century.* San Francisco: Berrett-Koehler Publishers, 1992.

Robinson, John. *Coach to Coach: Business Lessons from the Locker Room.* San Francisco: Pfeiffer, an imprint of Jossey-Bass Inc., 1995.

> Robinson provides a clear and vivid explanation of how to develop leadership vision and a cohesive team focused on the vision.

Schneider, William. *The Re-engineering Alternative: Making Your Corporate Culture Work for You*, New York, Irwin One, 1994

This book builds on the Myers-Briggs typologies, when describing corporate cultures. It describes the strengths and vulnerabilities of such organizations.

Videos

The Leadership Challenge, CRM Films, 1990 (1-800-421-0833)

This is a 26-minute film featuring James Kouzes and Barry Posner, authors of the book by the same name. The film features four cases which are used to illustrate the five leadership practices (or characteristics). This is an excellent film to reinforce many of the concepts presented in this sourcebook.

Leadership in Action, CRM Films, 1990 (1-800-421-0833)

This is a 17-minute film featuring Bill Spencer and "the Antron Army" at DuPont. It illustrates leadership in action, particularly "Questioning Groupthink," "Resetting Direction," and "Guiding Cooperative Action." James Kouzes and Barry Posner provide a commentary. The story is engaging and the results impressive. This film provides an up-beat example of the impact of positive leadership.

Leadership and the New Science, CRM Films, 1993 (1-800-421-0833)

A 23-minute film on Margaret Wheatley's book of the same name (San Francisco, Berrett-Koehler Publishers, Inc., 1992) which builds on the self-organizing tendency of nature as seen in the "chaos theory." For those afraid of risk taking this can be a reassuring message.

The Power of Vision: Discovering the Future (1990) and *Paradigm Pioneer* (1992), Courthouse Learning Corporation (1-800-328-3789)

Both films feature Joel Barker who explains how our paradigms influence our openness to new ideas and how our willingness to question conventional wisdom can create major advances in human knowledge and corporate effectiveness.

Assessments

Social Style by David W. Merrill, Ph.D., Denver: The TRACOM Corporation

Those familiar with the Social Styles instruments used with many of the Wilson Learning training programs are familiar with this type of assessment. Merrill was the originator of that instrument. TRACOM is the company that Merrill heads.

Myers-Briggs Type Indicator by Katherine C. Briggs and Isabel Briggs Myers, Palo Alto: Consulting Psychologists Press, Inc.

> This mother and daughter team are the originators of what may now the most widely used personality-type assessment in business settings. These types are compatible with Jungian types. Certification to use is required.

Leadership Practices Inventory (LPI) by James Kouzes and Barry Posner, San Francisco: Pfeiffer, an imprint of Jossey-Bass, 1993

> An excellent and inexpensive assessment tool designed for administration in 360 mode. It is available in a team or individual format. A scoring program is also available.

Glossary

analogy—make a point by stressing the partial similarity between two *dissimilar* things, e.g., the *heart* and a pump, *adult* and *children's* behavior.

autonomy—the expectation that someone will freely decide on the correct course of action. The person may choose to consult with another opinion, but that decision is their own. They are not constrained to do so.

credit—providing positive feedback, one of the most motivating of extrinsic motivators. In crediting individual performance, leaders are careful to be credible. A credible source is one who demonstrates a knowledge of the specifics of an event and can describe the significance of the event in the context of a larger picture.

credible source—one who demonstrates a *knowledge* of the specifics of an event and can describe the *significance* of the event in the context of a larger picture.

*extrinsic reward*s—people are also rewarded by others for doing things. This is the extrinsic reward.

intrinsic reward—a task is intrinsically motivating when it provides its own reward.

lead—root of the word means "to go." A leader's vision takes followers to their destination.

leaders—people with a mission or vision, pioneers, those who inspire and encourage, often leading us to accomplish our personal best. They are motivated. Usually they have strongly held principles, which guides their actions. Being goal-oriented and principle-centered, they are agile in adjusting tactics to accommodate unforeseen obstacles that block them. How they get to the goal is not as important as the goal itself.

metaphor—describes one thing *as* or *in terms of* another, e.g., "A mighty fortress is our God," "A torrent of abuse...," etc.

paradigm blindness—Joel Barker describes this as a tendency to perceive what we expect to perceive and the inability to notice or take seriously phenomena outside our expectations. He cites examples of inventions—xerography, the quartz watch, which challenged the status quo and were ignored or rejected by those to whom they were shown.

personal power—the power followers freely bestow on a leader, because of the leader's *vision, values,* or *personal characteristics.* We call this *referent power.*

position power—the legitimate power which comes with a position—to reward or coerce. Many leaders are promoted to positions of power, where a certain level of "command" is bestowed on them as a result of that position. Many people abuse this power.

psychological hardiness—the ability to handle change and stress.

referent power—see *personal power*.

simile—compares two unlike things, uses the word *like*, e.g., "She is like a rose."

vision—vivid picture of both a *future destination* and the *journey along the way*. It is rich in detail and feeling. You know what it will look or sound like, and how it will feel, what it will be like to reach the destination. Instead of *vision*, many prefer to use words such as: *goal, mission, objective, calling,* or *personal agenda.*

Index

A

activities
    learning 7
    major 9
    supporting 9
activity
    constructive feedback 160
    crediting 162
    favorite things 142
    figures of speech 140
    finding people's preferences 153
    life path 138
    preferences 152
    risk taking 156
    signaling 158
    values 145
    vision 149
    visualization 154
Anderson, Terry 13
assessment
    celebration 185
    goal setting 179
    information gathering 182
    leadership characteristics 180
    listening 174
    paradigm 170
    tools 7
autonomy & control 129

B

Barker, Joel 20
Bennis, Warren 13
Blanchard, Ken 13, 126
building blocks 4

C

camaraderie
    building 134
camera-ready 3
celebrate success 134
celebration

assessment 185
certificate of achievement 55
certificates
    duplicate 42
    executive awards them 42
Clifton, Don O. 126
coaching
    assessment 176
    tailoring 126
    worksheet 127
Covey, Stephen 13
credibility builder 132
crediting
    activity 162
    credible 132
    effort & risk taking 132
    effort, risk taking 31
    steps 30
Csikszentimihalyi, Mihialy 130

D

diversity
    defined 190, 191, 192, 193, 195, 196,
        197, 199, 200

E

environments
    challenging 17
    entrepreneurial 18
    high-control 17
extrinsic
    vs intrinsic 29

F

facilitation & administration 5
fair-mindedness 118
favorite things activity 142
fear
    over-generalizing 118
feedback 130
figures of speech
    activity 140

followership
    creating 15

G

generalize 20
Ghandi, Mohandas Karachand 113
goal setting
    assessment 179

H

Handy, Charles 17, 115
Herse, Paul 126
Hirsh, Sandra Krebs 17, 115

I

icons
    explained 9
images
    are everywhere 141
information gathering
    assessment 182
intrinsic *see* extrinsic

K

King, Martin Luther 24, 112
Kotter, John 24
Kotter, John P. 13
Kouzes & Posner 13, 19
Kummerow, Jean M. 17, 115

L

leader
    environments 115
    personality styles 17
    power source 16
    types 115
leader characteristic
    ability to visualize 110
    coach 27
    communicate 110
    curiosity 19, 117
    delegate 26
    empathy 120
    encourage initiative 26
    fear 21

initiative 20
inspire others 25
openness 20, 110, 117
repeats vision 123
set/maintain standards 31
sets example 28
leader skills
    build camaraderie 32
    celebrate milestones 32
    communicating 18
    credit 30
    interest 120
    listening 119
    respect individuality 30
leaders
    as communicators 18
leadership
    and management 116
    assess 167
    assessment 174
    characteristics 5, 6
    organization 11
    recognizing 113
    why 11
leadership characteristic
    assessment 180
life path
    activity 138
listening
    assessment 172
    skills 119

M

Merril model 16
Myers-Briggs assessment model 16
motivation
    extrinsic 130
        vs intrinsic 29
    intrinsic 130
motivators
    crediting 131
    intrinsic 131

N

Nelson, Paula 126

O

openness
over-generalizing 118
organization
change 11
efficiency 11
over-generalizing 20, 118

P

paradigm
assessment 170
paradigm blindness 117
paradigm blindness/awareness 20
Peters, Tom 13
position power
defined 16
power
personal 16
position 16
referent 16
preferences
activity 152
finding people's 153
psychological hardiness 118

R

resources
recommended 3
responsibility
sharing 125
ridicule 26
risk taking
activity 156
roleplay
constructive feedback 160
crediting 162

S

Schneider, William 17, 115
session
announce 40
checkoff list 43
endorsement 42
executive lunch 42
invitation letter 40

invitations 40
preparation 42
room setup 48
signaling
activity 158
skills
and talents 125
define 125
standards 133
stereotyping 118
subject/chapter matrix 5, 13
subject/reference matrix 5
supervision
basics 5

T

team
encourage members 29
training 128
team member
strengths 125
Teresa, Mother 112
Thoreau, Henry David 113
time block matrix 7
time block/methods matrix 7
training plans
navigating 8

V

values
activity 145
vision
activity 149
attracts 22, 122
building 22, 122
communicate it 23
communicating 123
developing 21, 121
examples 24
forms 23
grow 22, 122
managing it 25
past influence 22
requires team 125
statement 23, 123
what it is 21, 121

vision statement
    its power 24
visualization
    activity 154
volatile
    environments 17

W

Williamson, Bobette Hays 125